Bootstrap Marketing

101 top tips for marketing your business on a budget

First published in 2012 by Bootstrap Publishing, The Stables, Rossholme, East Brent, Somerset, TA9 4JA

This edition first published in 2012 by Bootstrap Publishing
info@bootstrappublishing.biz

www.bootstrappublishing.biz

Copyright ©2012 Mike Morrison
ISBN: 978-1-4710-8962-6

About the author

I must admit that in the first draft of this book, this particular section was written as "Mike is a 28 year old entrepreneur..." – however the pain of writing about myself in the third person was simply too much to bear. I'm not really one for all of the fluff and nonsense that is typical of so many things in business, so let's do away with that right now shall we?

I've had a fascination and a strong passion for creativity, business and marketing for as long as I can remember, and particularly love marrying the three together. I set up my very first online business at the age of 14, and after that first £1.34 hit my bank account I was hooked. Creating something out of nothing became a hobby of mine, and so while friends were out playing football, I was running my own little lawn-mowing operation trimming the gardens of people in my village; and while the kids at school organised table tennis tournaments, I was there building websites, designing flyers and whipping up a crowd so I could take bets on who would win each game.

From running Young Enterprise ventures to setting up an unofficial college tuck shop (pro tip: gorging on your own stock is bad for business), the entrepreneurial spirit followed me through everything I did growing up, spurred on by my own particular style of marketing and getting noticed. All of this provided far more value than what I was being taught about business and marketing in the classroom and lecture halls.

Even during my detour into the world of "normal" employment, my passion for marketing and business remained and shone through in everything I did, eventually leading to me starting my own businesses and applying everything I'd learned in a real world environment.

Funny thing is, despite the fact I'd be running my own little online and offline businesses for years; the second I started something "legit" (or, to put it another way, "conventional"), everything I'd learned seemed to disappear into nothingness. I've heard it said that an expert is someone who has made all of the mistakes it's possible to make in their field; and boy did I make some hefty mistakes in those formative years of running my first business.

Importantly though, I learned from them and used those missteps to progress my understanding of small business marketing, particularly when such things as a "marketing budget" is an alien concept.

I now run several successful businesses, have worked with a range of big name international brands, but more importantly have had even greater fulfilment working with other small businesses in order to help them improve their marketing both online and offline, to great effect.

I'm passionate about taking what I've learned over the last 15 years and using that to help other people to do what I've always loved doing – creating something from nothing; and when I'm not doing that I particularly love writing and speaking to anyone who will listen about all the different angles of what I call "Bootstrap Marketing".

On the personal side of things there's not a huge amount to say – I'm a huge geek, big time film fanatic, seldom read anything that isn't related to what I do, and harbour a secret yearning to one day figure out how to play golf. After living in Newcastle all of my life, I've recently moved to the South West, where I live in a quaint little country village with my very patient and understanding partner (and her mad cat), who no longer gets frustrated at my rants about my inability to find anywhere selling Stotties or Pease Pudding.

Before I finish fawning over myself I just wanted to share this one small thing. My favourite module of the business course I studied in college was, predictably, marketing – helped by the fact it was delivered by one of my favourite teachers. Imagine my dismay when my favourite teacher wrote in my school report that despite my obvious aptitude and ability, I would "never make anything of myself unless I could be pried away from the Internet".

So Mr. Redshaw, this one is for you!

Contents

Introduction

One of the things I love most about marketing small businesses is how agile they can be in terms of being able to navigate and adapt to an ever-changing world. It's not uncommon, however, to come across companies who seem stuck in the mud when it comes to their marketing strategy.

It's almost as though there's some sub-conscious notion that we must stick to whatever we wrote in our initial business plans – that the products or services we set out to sell are set in stone, and if people aren't buying then we need to try harder – and I've seen companies go under solely due to their resistance to move with the market.

I was never a sporty kid, but one game I did like was Dodgeball – I'm sure you're played it – it's state sanctioned assault conducted with hard rubber balls. Cast your mind back to those P.E sessions at school and those frantic games of Dodgeball... if you stood there, dazzled like a rabbit in headlights, rooted to the spot and unable to move then you were guaranteed to get hit, hard...

However if you stayed on your toes, dodged and weaved around all incoming obstacles and stayed alert then you stood a better chance of survival – what's more you could find yourself with the ball in your hands, at which point you could survey your surroundings, pick your opportunities, and take a shot. This alone didn't guarantee you'd hit your target, but you stood a much better chance of doing so than you would if you were sat on the sidelines.

That's as good an analogy for small business as you're likely to get out of me, but a fitting one I feel. As small business owners we are perfectly positioned to be leaner, more nimble, and more adaptable than larger companies, however far too often we don't take advantage of this.

The main reason? Money. Marketing costs money, and in most small businesses money doesn't come cheap. However I've got news for you – that's not a reason, it's an excuse, and one which it's becoming increasingly difficult to hide behind.

This is where the Bootstrap mentality is born. Forget the idea that you need to spend big to get results, and instead pull yourself up "by your bootstraps" and get to work on taking action in order to drive results.

I wrote this book to help people in danger of becoming stuck in the mud; who look at marketing as an expensive exercise and as such make the mistake of ignoring it. The world has changed, the opportunities are there just waiting to be grasped; and through this book I hope to help others take advantage of them.

This isn't a theory-filled textbook; it's somewhat rough around the edges, and I make no apologies for not pulling my punches. If you want flowery language and theory models then I can direct you to half a dozen appropriate books on Amazon.com. If, however, you want no-nonsense, down to earth advice and actual results, then this is the book for you.

The Basic Stuff

Often when people are first starting out in business, there are so many different things to take care of that it's easy to be shoved past the basics and thrown right into the deep end. More often than not when this happens, we find ourselves so embroiled in the day to day "stuff" that we get further and further from establishing the grounding we need in some of the core elements of running a business.

This is certainly the case when it comes to marketing, and it's not uncommon to turn important activities such as planning and developing a website, writing content for a brochure or designing a business card into tasks on a to-do list; without any real thought, strategy or understanding behind them.

Unless you have a background in marketing then this is understandable; but believe me even those who do have that background make the same mistakes!

The aim of this section is to address some key basics of marketing, branding and more. Whether it's addressing your mindset when it comes to sales and marketing; getting you to think about things you take for granted like your company name, business cards; or outlining some pitfalls to avoid – this selection of tips has been chosen to things started without the need for you to bore yourself to death with a textbook thicker than your leg.

So, without further ado, let's get started...

Understand what marketing really is

1

I suppose we can't really delve into advice on marketing without first establishing what marketing is, and making sure that this remains in the forefront of your mind in the day to day running of your business.

There are hundreds of extremely thick textbooks, college and university courses, audio books, DVDs, conferences and training courses out there all geared around explaining what marketing is, so I'm going to do you a favour and sum all of that up in just 3 words...

Marketing is everything.

Okay, so my job is done, let's end the book there... Maybe not eh? Of course like everything that simple there's a hell of a lot more to it, but the key to getting a firm grasp on what marketing your business entails is to understand that it relates to everything about what you do, and every message your customers receive about your company - literally, metaphorically, direct, indirect, purposefully or accidentally.

It's your logo, your website, the way you answer your phone (and whether you answer it at all), your prices, the quality of your work, how friendly you are, the way you dress, whether you put little kisses at the end of emails - every conceivable way in which your business enters the lives and minds of others, is marketing.

The core tenants are the "4 p's" - People, Product, Price and Promotion, and over the years there have been a whole bunch of other P's added to the mix too (Place, Personality,   Pepperoni...), but ultimately it does all come back to what I said previously - marketing is everything.

Not only is marketing everything you do, it is also everything to your business too, as without getting your marketing right, your business cannot ever truly get off the ground for any sustainable period of time. If your products are wrong, your customer service is rubbish, your logo has been hand-drawn in crayon or you fumble to explain what it is that you do then your business will suffer for it.

You can get by with marketing which is just "okay", but in doing so you're not enabling your business to reach its full potential. If your marketing is just outright terrible, then it's only a matter of time before you're stacking shelves in Asda.

You can't feed your family with theory, so for the most part I'm going to stay away from too much textbook stuff throughout this book, favouring practical stuff instead - however the single most important thing I need you to take away is the importance of marketing and the fact that, say it again with me one more time... Marketing is everything!

An hour a day

2

I have to admit, I've been guilty of uttering the words "there aren't enough hours in the day" more than a few times, and often this is the excuse people give for not focusing enough time on their marketing. Typically we all get so carried away with doing the grunt work in our business that we don't make enough time for working on the business itself.

I'm not the right person to get into time management techniques, but the first piece of advice I'd give you is to not count marketing as a separate, disposable activity. If you look at it this way then it will always play second fiddle to the influx of other tasks which inevitably land on your desk.

That's easier said than done, of course, and so my second bit of advice would be to specifically take an hour or more out of every day where you will work on nothing but marketing your business. This doesn't mean you don't market at other times, but for that hour, you commit to only working on the stuff that will win you new clients.

I'm an early riser so typically I get up at 6.30, spend an hour reading, writing and planning my day, then the following hour working solely on marketing. That means I actually get quite a lot done before 8.30 at which point I get sorted and head to the office.

I'd struggle to believe anyone who tells me that they can't afford to take a single hour out of every day to do this - so if you're struggling to find time to focus on marketing, try doing this for a week and keep note of how much you get done, I'm certain you'll find it infinitely more effective than what you're doing now!

Don't just sell, sell, sell

3

Sales are the lifeblood of any business and are, ultimately, the desired end result of all of our efforts. There's no disputing nor hiding from that fact; however some people are so hell-bent on reaching that goal in the quickest possible time that they inadvertently shoot themselves in the foot.

It's a fair guess that many of you reading this may be married, or at least have known someone in their lives who is married. How many of those marriages came from one party throwing a ring at the other the first time they met them?

I'm sure if you're anal enough you could find me a handful of examples where that has happened, but by and large there's a lot which has to come first. Getting to know someone, romancing them, taking them to fancy restaurants, pretending to like their parents etc - there's a process involved, one which varies from couple to couple, but still a process nonetheless.

You can't rush, harass, bully or trick someone into a sale - okay, you can, but then they haven't bought anything, they haven't bought you or your product; you've just sold to them by ramming your sales "technique" down their throat. Will that person buy from you again? Will they recommend you to friends or talk about you in a positive light?

Modern marketing focuses much more on relationships and engagement than "traditional" marketing, and nowhere is that more prevalent than in the world of small business; attempting to bypass that is foolish and makes you stick out like a sore thumb. Small businesses in general are fairly insular - we build up networks around us that are relatively small, and we share a lot with them. You can be damn sure that if you rub someone up the wrong way by being "that" person who is always trying to hard-sell then they'll tell their networks all about you.

Focus on developing relationships, establishing rapport, communicating and engaging with your market and you'll find that the sales opportunities open up for you. That's not to say that you should never try to sell, or that sales is a dirty word, just that you need to recognise that a sales "process" is just one piece of the puzzle. Ignoring that will find you quickly becoming the person who everyone tries to avoid at networking events, whose calls they automatically send to voicemail, and whose email they delete without a seconds thought.

Nobody wants to be "that" guy!

Feed the pipeline

4

Very few marketing activities result in instant gratification, however so many business owners wait until times get a bit tight before they'll go out and market their business.

Marketing can't be a completely reactive thing, and certainly isn't a measure of last resort! The phrase "make hay while the sun shines" really does apply here; if you're busy and enjoying a steady flow of work then this is the time when you should be marketing, in order to ensure your good fortune continues. It's also more likely that if the business is doing well you'll be more positive, motivated and creative when it comes to marketing, as well as having more financial resources to make your ideas happen.

Defensive marketing is not a good practice to get into, instead, consider the idea of a marketing "pipeline" - where what you put in today, in terms of your marketing activity, will only start coming out of the "other end" - i.e. generating results, in a few months time.

If you're spending all of you time on defensive marketing techniques and chasing quick wins, then you are just delaying the inevitable as the "pipeline" isn't being "fed" with solid, longer term activity.

So, whatever you do, make sure you are continuously feeding your marketing pipeline.

Don't let technology make you lazy

5

You know what I miss far more than a relatively sane 28 year old should miss? The little toys you used to get in the bottom of cereal boxes. Where did they go? Seriously!?

These days it's all about scanning the QR code on the back of the box to be taken to a link where you have to submit mailing details in order to enter a contest. Personally, I preferred the little figurines of Tony the Tiger in a variety of seductive poses.

Frosties fantasies aside, you used to always be able to rely on soft drink manufacturers to give you a fun contest to go with your 3000 calories of sugary goodness - whether it was collecting red ring pulls (I can never remember what for, yet I had a collection of hundreds of the bloody things), or finding a "WIN" printed underneath one. Now you just get a 6 digit code which you have to text to a premium rate number.

Remember when Walkers crisps hid ten pound notes in their packs? I found one of those back in the days before that £10 would be just enough to buy yourself another packet of crisps. Now you have to peel open the packet for a code to enter on their website.

There is a point to this aside from highlighting that I eat way too much rubbish, and that is that technology seems to have made a lot of marketers very lazy, bland and unimaginative. There are examples to the contrary, of course, but it does seem like a lot of the joy has been sapped from the sort of stuff I've described here.

Or maybe it's just me getting older, I don't know, I just know that my younger cousins and their friends aren't hanging around in the school playground exchanging QR codes.

What's in a name?

6

Many people confuse branding with the logo or the name of the company. While this is not the case, these things act as the mental "shortcut" through which you help to conjure up the wide range of emotions someone associates with you and your business, as such they are very important.

Despite this there are so many companies where it seems the name was something of an afterthought, and typically leads to them simply blending into the background.

This tip is possibly wasted on you as chances are most people reading this book will already be in business, but maybe it will give you pause for thought. It pays to apply a little creativity to your choice in company name for a variety of reasons:

- A unique company name increases the likelihood that an appropriate domain name will be available
- If you register as a limited company you must do so with a name nobody else has taken, so "5 Star Taxis" and the like won't cut it
- People remember unique names
- Generic company names tend to be longer ("Surrey Fencing Services") - making it harder to build a design, such as your logo or website, with any level of creativity

There are arguments to be made for using a generic or obvious name - nobody is going to get confused about what "ABC Accountants" do; however if your company name and brand are boring and bland then the assumption will be that you are too! There is no real reason why a description of what you do needs to be a part of your company name. "Apple" works better than "Apple Computers and Multimedia Devices";

"Nike" works better than "Great Trainers Inc"; "Tesco" works better than "UK Grocery Stores Limited" - get the picture?

Of course you don't want to go so far "out there" that your choice of company name becomes wildly inappropriate... "Fun-for-all Funerals" might be a bit of a hard sell, but being sensible, spending time to think through your company name and applying a little bit of creativity can go a long way.

Register your company?
The marketing implications

7

You know when you buy a packet of peanuts and wonder what sort of person made what type of complaint to elicit such an obvious statement as "may contain peanuts" on the back? Well, for that "sort of person" I'm going to preface this next bit by saying that I am in no way qualified to advise on the sort of legal structure you should choose for your business. Sole trader, limited company, partnership, etc, they all have different legal, liability and tax implications; and while I'm certainly well educated in the different choices by no means am I providing business or tax advice here!

Instead I'm going to focus purely on the marketing side of things, in terms of how the varying perceptions of your business structure can affect your ability to win business.

I'm going on the assumption that a large number of people reading this will be sole traders, rather than a limited company, and not registered for VAT. To some, "sole trader" is a bit of a dirty phrase as it gives something of a "temporary" impression, or one of unreliability. I dare bet every sole trader reading this has heard the words "yeah but it's not a real business though, is it", or something to that effect, from someone who has never been in business for themselves and has no real clue what they're talking about.

The negative connotations of being a "small fish" can often make people rush to register their company to validate themselves as a business owner. While that's not the best reason to do it, there are undoubtedly benefits in appealing to larger clients by appearing larger and more "legit" yourself. Having your company number in the footer of your website and your VAT registration on invoices tells people you're a real company and that you're not just going to disappear off the face of the earth.

Of course that's a fallacy, but when talking purely about the impression it gives it's hard to deny it's of benefit in a lot of cases.

On the other side of that though, if your market consists of other small businesses who themselves aren't limited nor VAT registered, then they may be put off if they think you're "big" (read: expensive), and of course they're not able to reclaim any VAT you charge them.

Ultimately from a marketing perspective I guess it comes down to who your client base is, and essentially trying to "match" the characteristics of your typical customer base. Being the only limited company in a sea of sole traders is just as negative from a marketing perspective as being the only unregistered business in a crowd of limited companies.

Keep in mind though that marketing and controlling perceptions should be a way down the list of considerations when it comes to making this choice, so be sure to speak to your accountant or business adviser if you're not sure which way to go.

Be your own designer

8

I'm sure that all of the professional graphic designers out there will be lining up to give me a piece of their mind after this one, but here I go anyway...

Depending on your particular type of business, you may benefit from some well designed leaflets and flyers, however with print costs as well as the cost of hiring a graphic designer, the risk to those working on a limited budget is off-putting.

Usually this results in the business owner cobbling something together in Microsoft Publisher, printing it off on their £19.99 Bubblejet printer and cutting them to shape with a pair of kitchen scissors.

There is a better way...

Fortunately these days there are cheap, and even some free, alternatives to Photoshop, the industry standard software for graphic design. These alternative programmes are improving all of the time, and make it far more feasible for anyone to produce something which looks a hell of a lot better than a few bits of clipart and some fancy fonts.

My personal recommendation would be Gimp, which is freely available from www.gimp.org and strikes an impressive figure against the far more expensive Adobe Photoshop.

While software alone does not make you a designer, it's a good place to start from. If you're looking to design leaflets, do a Google search for "leaflet design tutorial", or something similar.

The results you produce will be nowhere near as impressive as if you'd paid a professional, but they would at least lose that obvious "home made" look that desktop publishing programmes give.

There is no substitute for real, solid quality design, but we're bootstrapping here, so no room for £500 invoices from designers!

Invest in your business card

9

I'm all for doing things "on the cheap" where you can when it comes to marketing, but one of the things I strongly advise you don't take the cheap route with is your business card. Business cards are passed around by the boxful in the course of our business lives, and we all end up with either a shoebox full of ones we've received, or a very full recycling box.

With that in mind it's important to have a business card which stands out. That doesn't mean having one shaped like a piggy bank (which people are less likely to keep and file properly since they're an awkward fit for card holders plus, y'know, they're tacky as hell.) You can make your card stand out through the quality of its design, and the quality of print.

It doesn't actually need to be expensive either. A decent business card design will likely run you up a few hours with a graphic designer, and 500-1000 double sided cards printed on good stock with some nice lamination (Matt lamination for understated, glossy for shinier finishes) shouldn't cost you more than £50.

Note I said double sided, because there's no greater waste than that of a single sided business card. You don't have a huge amount of space to work with, so why limit that further by only focusing on one side? Maximise the available space for your logo, contact details and a list of services you offer.

There will, of course, still be people who throw your card in the bin, and that's unavoidable, but a good quality, professional business card can sometimes work wonders and can make people take a bit more notice of what you're all about.

If you do invest in your business card, make sure you have plenty of them, and that you always keep some on you - being caught card-less is embarrassing; particularly if it means you miss out in an opportunity!

Even if you don't invest in your business card, please do me a personal favour, no matter how bad things get, never ever order the free business cards from Vistaprint, they're just embarrassing...

Brandless branding

10

As previously mentioned, branding is one of the most misunderstood elements of modern business, particularly in the SME market. People often confuse a logo design or a tagline with "branding" when in fact they are just visual shortcuts to a range of thoughts, emotions and experiences which encompass a company's brand.

However, most of us cannot afford to bring in a brand consultant, in fact a lot of us will not have hired a professional designer to create our logo and thus establish some of the basics of the brand.

So, on that notion, let's look at one of the easiest ways to establish brand consistency when you don't have a clearly defined brand.

The simplest way, is with colour. Namely, the colours of your logo

I used to work for a company whose name included the word "scarlet". It was the MD's favourite colour and as such was a big part in the branding of the company. The MD always wore a red coat, red lipstick and red fingernails, all female employees wore red blouses, all male employees red ties, all chairs in the office were red, red lever arch files, red letter trays, red screen dividers - everything as red as possible.

Every time a client came in and sat down on the red sofas it was something they remarked on. The strength and consistency of that one colour helped to add a little extra gloss onto the professional image of the company, and provided a greater level of depth and presence to the overall brand.

My friends at Orangetree Development (www.orangetreedevelopment. co.uk) do the same too. Their brand is (surprisingly) built around the colour orange; and as you may expect the walls of their office are painted orange, matched by the colour of their chairs, stationary etc. Even tiny little touches such as the fact that when posting on online forums, they colour the text of their posts orange too.

Does your brand make good use of colour, and is it something you could take further? You don't need to be a walking business card, but if you're comfortable extending your brand with little touches and quick wins then it's certainly worth considering.

Avoid over-thinking your logo

11

This is something which the majority of small businesses I come across fall foul of; over-thinking and overdoing their logo.

Whilst we've established that branding isn't just about your logo, it is still an important element, and all too easy to get wrong. Your logo should, essentially, be shorthand for all of the things which someone associates with your company – however if it's too complicated, nonsensical or downright ugly then people will end up getting lost in the technical side of figuring out your logo rather than getting swept away with the emotions and experiences it should represent.

I'm not quite sure why many business owners over-cook this. Perhaps it's just being over-enthusiastic; perhaps it's inexperience or a lack of creativity; or maybe it's a sense that the value and tangible aspects of a logo are directly linked to the number of elements it contains.

The important thing to keep in mind (and this applies to most things in your business), is that you're not the audience you're aiming at – and as such your personal tastes or preferences pale in significance compared to the things which will appeal to your potential customers.

Just take a look at some of the most well known logos out there:

Nike: a simple "swoosh"
McDonalds: A pair of yellow arches making up the letter "M"
Apple: A straightforward shape of an apple

You don't even need a symbol or icon in order to have an effective logo; think of brands such as Marks & Spencers – their logo consists solely of a nice font in their corporate colour – however you recognise it and associate with it instantly.

The right selection of font and colour can sometimes be all you need as a basis for your logo; and this is helpful for a Bootstrap approach because it means that – with a bit of thought – you could create something yourself! I've seen some logo's which were "designed" in Microsoft Paint which looked better than ones which have been created by a professional subject to the crazy demands of their client!

The last thing you want to be doing is constantly chopping and changing your logo, so it's important to get it right early on. As such you don't want to rush it, and similarly you shouldn't overcomplicate it to the point where it's a steaming mess!

Cobbler's shoes

12

Of all the tips and advice in this book, this is the one I'm most guilty of not following; which is ironic given that it revolves around following your own advice!

Fortunately it's only relatively mild - as someone who runs a web design company I of course have a website - however I know I don't use this as effectively as I could, and I've actually hated the bloody thing since the day after it went live. Years on and I've only just settled on a redesign which addresses the problems and have finally found the time to update the site, to great reception and an almost instant increase in enquiries. Aside from the website I also help people get great results with email marketing, yet don't send my own campaigns nearly enough as I should. Same goes for SEO, blogging etc.

It's a condition known as "Cobbler's Shoes" - based on the idea of a cobbler being so busy fixing other peoples shoes that his own end up full of holes.

Believe it or not I have actually come across web designers who don't have a website! More commonly there are those who use Wordpress with pre made templates which other people have designed! It's not just the web design industry, I've come across debt advisors who are on the verge of bankruptcy, sales coaches whose businesses go under due to lack of sales, and even hugely overweight personal trainers!

Essentially all this tells people is that your service or product doesn't work, and that the promises you make about how you can positively impact their business or lives are empty ones. A chef who won't eat his own food sends a very bad message, and if you won't "buy" what you're selling, why should anyone else?

Don't compete, collaborate!

13

I mention 4networking - the UK business networking organisation - a fair bit in this book as it's played a large part in so many aspects of my personal and business life; however before I joined 4Networking, I was a card-carrying member of their "rival" of sorts - BNI.

For anyone unfamiliar with BNI, it's an organisation based on passing referrals, something which requires a strong set of rules in order to facilitate members within each "chapter" generating leads for each other. One of those rules is an industry "lock-out", which means only one person from an industry can be represented in each chapter. So within your group you're the only web designer, printer, accountant etc, and your "spot" is "protected" for as long as you keep paying your membership. In theory this means if anyone in the group comes across an opportunity for someone in your industry, you're the only person they'll pass that lead to.

It's a format which undoubtedly works well for some people, and it did for me, but I quickly became jaded with what were, at times, very restricting rules that didn't seem to serve me or my business well, and so I started looking for somewhere else to eat breakfast. Enter 4networking.

February 2009, I attended my very first 4networking breakfast meeting. Keeping in mind that I'd been accustomed to being the only person in my industry within the room for over a year; Imagine then my horror with the first person I met at 4N being another bloody designer! And what's worse, he did website design too, which was my particular area of expertise! I genuinely almost turned around and headed home before the meeting started, but the walk back to the car was highly visible and I couldn't muster the courage or come up with a good excuse, so I stuck around.

Years on and we've collaborated on a good number of projects, putting our complimentary skill-sets together to not only deliver improved quality services to clients but also to give them more options than we have been able to offer on our own.

Having my mind opened to the concept of collaborating instead of competing has reaped dividends, and I've had the pleasure of working with a number of other web agencies and freelancers all over the UK. So, words to the wise, set aside your conventional view of competitors, and start looking for collaborative opportunities instead.

Too good to be true

14

I remember in my early days of freelancing I received a call from an excitable young man. Having an embarrassing amount of free time on my hands, and despite knowing this was a sales call, I decided not to put the phone down, but to indulge him a little.

Shortly into the call I forgot myself, and found that I was becoming swept up in what this guy was saying. He was a salesperson for yell.com and as a new business wanted to talk about how he could help me. He reeled off some stats about how my free ad on their site had been doing, and then started asking me about things like my average job size, the sort of client budgets I'd like to be working with, and what my capacity was in terms of how many projects I could take on a month. This all tied back to him "tailoring" an ad deal for me to have a paid listing on their site, on the basis of it bringing me X amount of work in accordance to my capacity etc.

Now, I have a sales and marketing background. I also have some seriously beefy Internet marketing chops, yet ladies and gents; I bought into this bloke and signed up to a yearlong agreement...

Shameful.

Of course it was all rubbish, I monitored the stats from the ad and not only did it not bring me any clients, it barely brought me any website visitors. Worst thing is that I wasn't surprised. I'd been sold to, and had gotten so carried away with the picture this extremely talented salesperson had painted me that not only did I forget everything I know about sales, marketing and web "stuff" but I also forgot a basic rule - if it sounds too good to be true, it probably is!

There are a lot of companies out there who specifically target small businesses; preying on the weaknesses and problems almost all of us have but few of us are prepared to concede - low confidence, poor sales, fear of failure, lack of knowledge etc - and so when they come riding in on their white horse with promises galore it is all too easy to get swept up in it all.

So keep your wits about you when someone approaches you with promises to get you to the top of Google, or has an eBook they're selling which unlocks the secrets to making £5000 a day, or a unique advertising opportunity etc as no matter how much you think you know or how confident you are that you won't be sucked in, it happens to the best of us!

Don't get carried away

15

I went a little overboard when I first started freelancing. I was convinced that in order to be taken seriously in business I needed to have a whole load of professionally printed promotional materials, and over a space of 3 months I spent close to £4,000 on leaflets, presentation folders, printed sales letters and all sorts of other stuff I didn't need.

Problem was I really didn't think it through, and I let myself be led by a "friend" who happened to be my printer.

And so I ended up producing two leaflets that essentially said the same thing, just at different sizes... 1000 of each. I ordered 1000 presentation folders in which I planned to store and send project documents such as proposals... 1000 of the things... I think I ended up using a dozen at most, and they cost me over £1000 (they also followed me through 3 house moves before being dumped in a recycling bin 4 years after I bought them). I ordered business cards, and two weeks later changed my mobile number; bought 1250 printed letterheads... Then moved office; ordered 2000 pre-printed sales letters which I never sent out... And so on and so on

I was so enamoured with this idea of having stuff professionally printed, and since I was designing them myself it was easy to do; so I ended up blowing what - to a one man band freelancer - was a small fortune on boxes full of items that all ended up going to waste.

It's very easy to get carried away. There are loads of people out there who are only too happy to help you part with your money, and it's not hard to allow yourself to be convinced that things like this are sound investments. Just make sure you think things through before opening your wallet and be certain that you actually need what you're buying.

Prices and products

Ah, prices and products – two of the "4 P's of Marketing", and the cornerstone of everything we do. Every business needs to sell or offer something – otherwise it's just people sitting around updating their Facebook status; and if you're not charging and making money, then you're a charity, a hobbyist, or the next client of a debt management company.

Often the products and services we offer as small business owners are the result of something we're particularly good at, enjoy or have an interest in. Many "one man bands" are practitioners, who set themselves up in business because they have a particular skill-set which they can leverage.

Maybe it's a hobby that you realised you can make money from, or perhaps it's something you used to be employed to do. Either way in most situations, the "business part" is typically something which comes a long time after we've got our teeth stuck into the product or service being offered.

So if you're an accountant, chances are you learned your craft elsewhere first and now you're essentially selling the same thing, just for yourself. If you're a self-taught website designer, you're still building the same websites you used to build in your spare time, only now you're being paid for them.

Or perhaps you're in the ever-increasing camp of people who are in business because they had no other choice. Whether you consider yourself "unemployable", were made redundant, or have some other reason why you can't work for someone else – chances are you may have had to "scramble" to figure out what your products, services and pricing are.

In most of these situations, products and pricing are decided upon very early – or are based on "the norm"; jotted down into a business plan, written up onto a website, set in stone forever more.

This can lead to people being rooted to the spot, unwilling and unable to be flexible with their product offering or their pricing plan, regardless of what's going on in their market or how their customer base is responding. The savviest businesses adapt, spot opportunities and react accordingly – not just within their marketing approach, but throughout the core of their business.

It's understandable why many struggle with pricing and products – this is an area in which we all seem to take the lead of our competitors; or adhere to this bizarre notion of doing things according to what is the "norm" of the market. Such a thing doesn't exist, in my view, and even if it does, tethering your business to what everyone else is doing is a crazy strategy to follow.

Break the rules, break the norms, listen to your market and stay nimble.

Being brave with pricing

16

Before I started as a freelancer, my career had been in the financial sector, managing an insurance sales team. I was reasonably well paid in the context of salaries offered by that company; and so when I began my freelance career, I looked back to what I'd been paid in that job as a basis for setting my new hourly rate.

To me, the £15 per hour I'd previously been earning was a big deal - it had been the highest wage I'd ever earned, and so I set my freelance rate at £25 an hour. Every time I thought about it I got a huge smile, patting myself on the back for earning such a great wage.

What I forgot, however, is that in my old job I was paid a salary no matter what I did - whereas now, I only made money for client work, meaning that £25 an hour I got paid for the 30 or so hours of "output" actually had to be stretched to cover the 80+ hours of "input" it required to run my business.

It took me almost a year to realise that, and when I did I was too nervous to put my rates up.

It actually took a friend from within the same industry to snap me out of it. She couldn't believe what I was charging, as it was very much at the low end of the pricing scale within my industry, so she dared me to double it for my next proposal. I did as she suggested, and could barely believe that the client didn't bat an eyelid, and in fact that my quote still managed to compare competitively to others their company had received. Needless to say, I adopted that rate going forward, and have increased it twice since in order to keep up with the changing industry.

It's very easy to get your pricing wrong when starting out - either through misconceptions such as the ones I experienced, or out of fear that you're not worth what you're charging and will lose customers. You need to bite the bullet and be brave with your pricing; don't undervalue yourself and your offering, and whatever you do, try not to get sucked into the trap of forever competing on price.

Turning services into products

17

They say we're currently in a service-led economy. Whether that is true or not, it is common that most SME's tend to specialise in offering a service as opposed to the manufacture and sale of tangible products. This presents a challenge.

Think about what was likely your first experience of sales "training", somebody holding up a pencil, and asking you to sell it to them. Most people mutter something about the colour of the pencil, or how sharp it was, before being verbally slapped down by their smug trainer, who would then go off on a meandering ramble about this mere pencil being an implement in the weaving of dreams and so on and so on.

Most of the sales training and experience that the majority of SME owners will have had is with products, yet we're trying to sell services. Sure the fundamentals are the same, but actually services are harder to sell. Now I'm sure there are some sales trainers out there disagreeing with this, but we are not you, and most of us can't afford you!

Services are difficult to sell because you can't show people a service, they can't hold it in their hands, feel the quality of it. You can't photograph a service to put it on your website, and as most services are sold on a payment-for-time basis you can't give a fixed price for your service either.

So, do we struggle on with the more difficult task of trying to sell services, or do we take the easier road, and turn those services into products?

This can mean different things to different people. If you're an accountant, you might package up services aimed at new businesses and sell them as a "start-up package"; similarly a fitness trainer may create a "Beach Body" package consisting of a set amount of a particular type of training.

It's not just about adding a fancy name and "wrapping" the appearance of a product around service-based content. There may be scope for adding actual physical products into your predominantly service-based offering – for example someone providing computer repair services would be mad not to stock and sell a range of accessories.

Finally you could look at information products – ebooks, DVD's, audio guides and the like which help to impart knowledge related to the service you provide. If you're a sales coach, where is your audiobook series? If you're a mortgage advisor, where's your book on getting on the property ladder?

So look at your own business, think laterally about what it is your business offers (and indeed whether you can expand on this), and examine the opportunities to productise your offering.

Low cost subscriptions

18

New Years Day 2007, and like many others around the world I was preoccupied with setting my resolutions for the coming year. Along with some specific goals I hoped to achieve was the reliable mainstay resolution to join a gym.

For once, I actually followed through on this, and signed up to my local gym a few days later. For 3 months I attended regularly as clockwork, but as ever, I started to taper off, and by the end of April my membership card began the long process of gathering dust on my shelf.

Every month thereafter I would check my bank statement, spot the £50 charge for gym membership, and make a mental note to cancel it. I did this for the following 2 years, and despite reminding myself every month I didn't actually get round to cancelling until 2009.

Had the gym charged me the full fee upfront I would never have joined, however £50 a month made it far easier to make the buying decision, and was an amount which was insignificant compared to other monthly outgoings, so cancelling it never took priority.

How many of you can relate to that situation? I'm betting a lot of you, however I'm betting far fewer of you have tried to capitalise on it for yourself.

Offering a subscription-based product or service could be a gold mine for your business - particularly if you're providing something which would otherwise be an expensive one-off investment. Not only does it make buying much more accessible, but people forget or put off cancelling until way past the point they finish using your product or service.

Major software providers are already taking note. Adobe, whose products can typically run into thousands of pounds in cost, have recently began offering their software on a monthly subscription basis.

This all becomes much easier, and potentially more lucrative if you're selling knowledge as a service. Business consultants, life coaches, marketing advisors etc who ordinarily sell their services in the form of one on one sessions, are finding that by preparing a wealth of written information, videos and resources and offering them through a paid membership site, they're able to do the work once and make money for it over and over again.

If you're not in a knowledge-transfer industry, spend a bit of time exploring where the possibilities lie for creating a subscription product for your business. It's not going to be possible for every type of business, but is certainly something worth considering.

Reasons to return

19

One of my all-time favourite marketing strategies has to be that which my local gym employs (not the same gym as in the previous tip, I hasten to add!). As someone who enthusiastically avoided any form of physical exertion for a great number of years, the biggest challenge I had every time I decided I was going to start using a gym was having the discipline and motivation to actually get up and go there regularly.

As such, every gym membership I took out ended up being cancelled a year or so later.

What this gym does, however, is very clever. In addition to actually being a fantastic gym, they also have an extensive selection of DVD's available for hire by their members. Hiring a DVD doesn't cost a penny, however the condition is that they must be returned the next day otherwise you're charged a daily late fee.

This, of course, serves the dual purpose of providing an attractive extra to gym members, as well as giving a very good reason to attend regularly.

It's a simple idea, but an extremely effective one which should prompt you to look within your own offering to try to identify ways in which you can give your customers an incentive to return to you.

Round peg, square hole

20

I've lost count of how many times I've heard people say "there's no point doing x, y, z - it's not right for my product/service/business". In principle I agree that it's a little pointless throwing time and money into a no-win marketing situation; but some people are too quick to write things off out of an assumption that the market they cater to won't buy your product.

More often than not the issue lies with the individual and their approach rather than the offering - but if it truly is an issue with the product not fitting the market, then why bother trying to shove a round peg into a square hole, when instead you could try selling square pegs...

Basically if people won't buy what you're selling, bring them something they will buy!

JAM Call Answering (www.jam.co.uk) is a perfect example of this approach. As one of the first ever call answering services in the UK, this family business had grown to an impressive size, typically dealing with large companies dealing with outsourced sales campaigns and customer services.

In 2009 they decided to get involved in business networking, an area typically populated with small business. While many of those small businesses do have big connections, developing a relationship strong enough to "gain access" to those larger companies can take a lot of time. Given the complete contrast in the type of market they were dealing with, initial reaction within the company was that it was something of a wasted effort -very few people in the room would utilise their core offering.

At this point a lot of similarly sized companies would simply write-off networking as an activity which "didn't work for their product" - however

JAM took a more innovative approach, put their heads together, and came up with a product specifically geared towards smaller businesses and micro businesses. Their "Answer" service (www.answer.co.uk), which offers pay-as-you-go call answering at £1 a call - much cheaper, more flexible and more accessible to small businesses than competing services - has gone on to become phenomenally successful. JAM has recently recruited their 300th client from just one networking organisation they're part of and they're picking up more and more clients every day. They've also been able to broaden their market for this product outside of their local area, spearheaded by their marketing manager Katie Millman, whose promotional trips to various parts of the UK have consistently resulted in a slew of new clients.

Instead of trying to cram the "square peg" of outsourced call centre services into this new and unfamiliar market, they had the savvy to look closely at that market, analyse what they would need, and tailor a product to suit them.

So if you're sitting there thinking that nobody will buy your £5000 widget, come up with a £50 widget instead. Otherwise you're going to be missing opportunities while sitting there waiting for your perfect market to just open up to you.

Offer a money back guarantee

21

This is probably the one tip in this book that will have you instantly either shaking your head or rolling your eyes, and believe me until earlier this year I would have done the same. The concept of offering a money back guarantee in a small business world where cash flow is fragile enough to begin with is a radical one, but it's not quite as dramatic a move as you may think.

First, the obvious benefit - giving someone a money back guarantee eliminates any risk they feel is associated with their buying decision. The greatest fear anyone will have when parting with their hard earned cash is that, despite all their due diligence and your convincing sales spiel, it won't work, and if that happens they've lost out financially. Being able to eliminate that risk is a very powerful tool in your arsenal.

Before you ask, yes, you do have to mean it and follow through for those who take advantage of your money back guarantee; however you'll be surprised at how few people will actually do that.

For a start if your product or service does what it should, then people won't have a reason to ask for their money back. Even if it doesn't then you'll find a great number of people are so adverse to creating a "fuss" that they won't bother (though it's always worth following up on all sales to check the customer is happy, as even if you don't have to give them their money back you don't want negative word of mouth out there).

It's absolutely essential that this guarantee is conditional, not so much so as to undermine it, but sensible enough to protect you and your business. So, for example, the customer should be able to demonstrate why they're not happy with what you've done and back that up with proof, and there should be an allowance for you to attempt to remedy their issues before giving their cash back. Additionally there should be a time window during which they can "claim", and of course if it relates to a tangible product then this needs to be returned in order for a refund to be issued.

Services are a little trickier since you can rarely "get back" what you've sold if someone asks for a refund; so you need to be very confident in what you're providing and also very clear on the conditions. There are way too many intangibles for me to have started offering this guarantee for web systems just yet, but I do offer it for Internet marketing consultancy. I offer 3x1 hour sessions, the first session is free, and if after they've had all 3 sessions the customer doesn't feel they've had value they can ask for their money back. However, this is dependent on them demonstrating that they have utilised the advice I'd given them and that they haven't had results. If they've done this and my advice hasn't worked then essentially I've failed them, so have no issue providing a refund. There are, of course, caveats to circumvent the "chancers", but so far I've only had to issue one refund, and it was a partial one, where even though my advice had been effective and therefore I wasn't obliged to give them their money back, it was less hassle to just refund them then it was to stick to my guns.

If you tread carefully, offering a money back guarantee could be the best marketing tool you employ. It won't be for everyone, and is a bit gutsy, but definitely something worth chewing over.

Always offer a budget option

22

This is something I started doing just over a year ago and honestly has been one of the best things I've done. I work a lot with bespoke projects and as such my quotes are variable depending on what the client needs. Initially if a client told me they thought my pricing was a bit out of their budget, I'd almost always end up bringing the cost down in order to win their business, even though I'd end up doing the same amount of work.

I put a stop to that after a client who was referred by someone I'd worked for previously told me, once his site was complete, that he'd been told by the guy who referred him to tell me it was too expensive, regardless of what my quote was, as I'd be guaranteed to knock a few hundred off.

And so I toughened up, and when a client asked about bringing the price down, I'd respond with "okay, let's see which of the features you've asked for that we can lose in order to lower the time and cost"; more often than not they didn't want to compromise on what they wanted or needed, and so accepted that I wouldn't either.

I still felt uncomfortable having that conversation, and so decided to do something to pre-empt it. On every quotation I sent out, I included a cost for what they'd asked for, but I also included a budget alternative - something which would do the basics of what they needed, without the bells, whistles and frills. Sometimes this would be, for example, using a pre made Wordpress template and some plug-in's, which would give them an end result that was "close enough" to their requirements.

What this did was to instil the mindset that if they asked for it to be cheaper, this budget option was the one I'd point them too. In a few instances the client chose the budget options, because they'd either underestimated how much they were asking for, or didn't realise that such a budget route could exist - but in most cases they went with the original quote. The beauty of it was that costs were based on the amount of time they needed me to work on their job, and so even if they took the budget option I was still making my full hourly rate as there was less work involved.

I've since taken this a step further and started including the "gold plated" option - the one they could have if budget wasn't an issue, with absolutely every fancy feature thrown in. While not everybody takes that option, some do, and for those who don't it puts the other two into perspective and naturally nudges people towards the middle option of the original quote. What it also does, is gives them food for thought over what they may want a year or so down the line as they continue the development of their website.

So take a look at your own product or service - can you split it into a standard and a budget offering? Could you stretch it to a "deluxe" version?

Just as an added tip since we're looking at quotes; when I started using the 3 options I also began including a contract and specific timescales in my quotes too, whereas before I waited for confirmation they wanted to go ahead. Essentially I prepared my proposal on the assumption that they would, of course, be going ahead. If they don't go ahead straight away then all I've lost is a couple of extra sheets of paper!

Best of both worlds

23

I've lost count how many times, while networking, I've heard people say "I need bigger businesses" or "the companies here are too small for me", and I'll admit something, I've said it to myself a number of times!

I'd always had this niggling feeling that my path to real success lay in working with bigger clients, on bigger projects, with bigger budgets; and so I pushed myself and my business in that direction and after a lot of hard work finally got what I wanted. I'd made it... I was working for national and international brands, on projects with a lot more zeros in the budget than I'd had before - success, right?

Well, not quite... Firstly with clients like this, the number of stakeholders and "voices" involved made the whole process a nightmare. They say that a zebra is a horse, designed by committee; however I'd never truly appreciated that saying until working on these sorts of projects. Secondly while the money was great, the projects took longer to complete - if I was paid £50,000 it was because it was £50,000 worth of work, not because someone decided to give me a bucket-load of cash for an afternoons graft. With that came the fact that any delays or issues in receiving payments had much greater implications on cash flow. Finally, I was working myself into the ground as these clients expect so much more of you - the line between work life and home life disappeared, I was grumpy, not sleeping well, not eating well, and stressed beyond belief.

Success?

It was only when doing a yearly review that I looked back on all of the clients I worked with, looked at the issues I'd faced, and finally managed to see the link between the two. This enabled me to make the decision to focus on the sort of clients and the sort of work I enjoy - and that is working with smaller businesses like my own. Not only is the sense of fulfilment greater, but the work is so much more fun, and the projects are smaller meaning I can take more on, which means if something goes wrong on one project, or a client doesn't pay me, it has minimal impact as I have other projects to fall back on.

Now that's something of a cautionary tale against falling into the trap of thinking "bigger clients" are a nirvana of sorts, however I'm not naive enough to think that this will dissuade people from following that mindset. However for those people I'd have to ask - why does it need to be one or the other? Why not have the best of both worlds and tailor your business to cater to both big clients and small ones?

I talk about JAM Call Answering elsewhere in this book and point them out as a great example of doing this - their core offering is to act as a complete outsourced call centre, assisting with sales campaigns etc for national brands. That's their "big ticket" item - however they also have a fantastic offering at the other end of the scale with their pay as you go call answering service, which directly appeals to small businesses.

Look at what you do and consider the different ends of the scale. If you're hunting bigger businesses, what is it that you can actually offer them? Is there a variation of that which you can make available for smaller businesses too?

It's also worth asking yourself a couple of key questions. Firstly, why do you need bigger businesses? Is it because what you're selling is unaffordable to smaller businesses? Is it because your offering is only suited to the activities of a large business? Or is it because you envisage them buying more "stuff" from you than a small business would?

The second key question is, why would a big business bother with you? Are you a big business or a one man band? Why should the MD of a multimillion pound company give you the time of day? What can you offer them that their current supplier can't? If you're a one man band, or a small business that's been running a year or two, why should a big company take on the risk that you may not be stable enough to service them?

Most people who hunt bigger businesses have no idea why they do it; they get too wrapped up in the concept of "bigger". When it comes to the crunch chances are that even if the product is great, a big company would not do business with them for various other reasons, such as the fact they're a small business and would possibly be seen as a risky prospect. There are plenty of ways to overcome this, such as partnering with other companies under an "umbrella" brand in order to come closer to the structure of a larger, more stable organisation.

Don't get me wrong, if you've thought it through and know that your strategy rests in acquiring larger clients then go for it; just don't write off smaller ones. Be smart; tailor your offering so that you can take advantage of both ends of the market, offering the personal touch of a smaller business while still having your line in the water for the big fish. It is entirely possible to have the best of both worlds, however if you're hell-bent on gunning for the big clients then you could well be missing a wealth of opportunities.

Dabble with discounts

24

I'm writing this particular tip just a few days after Christmas, and now the excitement of receiving the '24' DVD box set has settled somewhat I've been desperately avoiding looking at what my favourite online stores have going on in the January sales.

I'm a sucker for a discount, and I'd bet you'd be hard pressed to find anyone who wasn't - what's not to like about saving money?!

Businesses harness this all year round, and it's something you could and indeed should do too.

It's a delicate balance, however - if people know that every other month you're going to be slashing prices then they will never buy something when it's at its full price; similarly, discounting your products or services regularly as a small business can give the impression that you're doing it because you're a bit skint!

If you run an online store, for example, with hundreds of products in stock then this isn't an issue; however chances are your product or service selection is relatively small due to the nature of what it is you do. As such I'd suggest some of these possible strategies:

Offer permanent discounts to certain groups of customers

If you're a member of a particular networking group, or you're heavily active on a particular website, forum or social media channel, then consider offering those customers a permanent discount - i.e. 10% off our fees for all Chamber of Commerce members; 15% discount for all of our Facebook fans and so on.

Give a discount for referrals

A great way to use discounts effectively is to offer them to people who refer new clients to you. i.e. refer a new client and receive 10% off your next invoice.

Discount multiple or repeat purchases

If you offer a lot of complimentary services or products, or ones which you would typically upsell "in sequence"; then consider tying a discount into your process to encourage multiple and repeat purchases. i.e. order a desk and get the chair half price, or get 10% off the price of hosting for your newly completed website.

Bribe customers with a discount

A great way to get more value out of discounting your products or services is to ask for something in return for giving it in the first place. For example, offer £5 off all purchases when people subscribe to your email newsletter, give you a testimonial, complete a survey or "like" your Facebook page.

Offer a discount for speedy payment

Cash flow is one of the most challenging things for small businesses, and there are few things more frustrating than sitting in wait for someone to pay their invoice. A novel idea would be to offer a 5% discount on invoices paid within 7 days of being issued. Of course in an ideal world this wouldn't be necessary as everyone would pay within hours of an invoice being received, but let's face it, that's a fantasy!

Give discounts for volume

If you charge by the hour this is a good one to consider - offering a discount for higher volume sales. For example a subcontractor I used on a recent project charged £45 an hour, but if we put him on retainer for 20 hours a month that rate dropped to £40 per hour.

Personally I offer tiered rates to retainer customers. If someone books me for a set number of hours on a month to month basis they pay my full rate; if they contract me on a 3 month cycle that rate drops by £5 an hour, it drops a further £5 an hour if I'm contracted for 6 months, and a further £10 if I'm put on a full year contract. Sure that drops my hourly earnings by up to £20, but the trade-off is the security of a fixed-term contract versus the uncertainties of being commissioned on a "pay as you go" basis.

Run limited special offers

If you want or need the flexibility of offering ad hoc discounts; be it a need to sell certain products, or a need to plug cash flow holes, then a good way to do this without giving off the wrong impression is to run offers with limitations. For example, half price widgets for the first 10 customers, 20% off for this weekend only etc.

That's just a handful of ways in which you can utilise discounting as part of your marketing strategy without cheapening your business or shooting yourself in the foot. If you're still not convinced, try running a small, limited discount offer to see how it goes - just remember to be smart about how you do it.

Going for gold

25

Just a quick one - if your service or product offering is available in a variety of packages, with tiered pricing according to the features, don't label these your "bronze, silver and gold" packages - use "silver, gold, platinum" instead.

This may just be a personal preference, but I find nothing appealing about choosing "bronze" - yet silver, gold and platinum all hold some appeal. Competitors who offer the same sort of tiered packages will likely go the bronze, silver, gold route; so your packages look that little bit better.

When you offer these types of tiered packages people most often choose the middle one - it makes them feel that they're getting value as they're not paying the top price, while also getting a good product as they're not choosing the basic one option - and so in that case, reassuring people that they made the right choice by calling it the "gold" package instead of the "silver" one is an easy win.

If you do offer services or products with these kinds of packages, consider switching it up a bit - it's a silly, small thing, but can have a strong effect.

Assume the position

I can't help but find irony in the fact that many large corporations spend an absolute fortune trying to capture the personality of smaller businesses, in an attempt to appear friendlier, more personal and approachable

When you consider this, the enormous opportunity presented to us as small business owners becomes clear. You can build elements of your marketing and positioning around your personality, rather than needing to employ brand specialists to "fake it" for you. You're able to go out there and represent your business, living and breathing its brand and character in a way larger companies simply can't.

It also means you can move and position your business quicker and more effectively; picking your spots within the market, being creative with how you operate and structure your business.

The fact that you can make your own decisions about who you are, what you do and where you stand; and more importantly can tweak and tinker your position as and when needed, gives you a lot of power and manoeuvrability unmatched by larger competitors.

So think hard about who you are and how you can marry your personality with that of your business. What's your place in the market? How do you stand out? Who are your customers? Where are your competitors? And how do you deal with them?

These are the things this section aims to cover. It's a big ol' market out there and it's up to you to pick your spot and firmly plant your flag – so go out there and make your mark!

Buck the trend

26

I'm a massive fan of Gary Vaynerchuk (www.garyvaynerchuk.com) who, in his book "Crush It" (absolute essential reading, by the way), explains how he went against the grain of a traditionally stuffy wine distribution industry and as a result massively increased not only his profits but his own personal brand.

While most wine aficionados would witter on about a particular tipple having a great body, and blabber something about tannins; Gary would record videos talking about how a certain wine tasted of burnt rubber and marmite, and he'd do so in an informal environment, wearing a t-shirt instead of a 3-piece suit and monocle.

He was, naturally, derided by others in that industry; however the people that mattered, his potential customers, lapped it up. More than that he made wine tasting and wine appreciation accessible to several demographics to which it had previous been just far too stuffy.

Gary is now celebrated for his business nous, creativity and social media savvy and in addition to being a bestselling author is in continuous high demand at a wide number of speaking events.

All because he bucked the trend of his industry and didn't fall into the trap of telling himself "well this is how it's supposed to be done".

Don't let others in your industry dictate how you should behave or market your business - rock the boat a little bit, try something new, upend assumptions and rebel against the perceived way things "should be done".

Don't ruin a good thing

27

It's often hard enough to get your message across to your market, but if that message changes with each passing day then the task becomes insurmountable. Despite this I often come across people who constantly chop and change their business. One week they're virtual assistants, the next week they're marketing consultants.

I empathise to some degree, particularly with young businesses or people new to being self employed, where there's a certain period of finding your feet. There are also common situations where your market ends up shaping your business into something different from what you originally planned. However there are definitely people who are so concerned with chasing the latest bandwagon in the hopes of making some fast cash, so concerned that they don't realise when they've got it good.

One particular person comes to mind for me. He's a long term member of a networking organisation I'm involved in, and over a period of 3 years I've seen him come and go with at least half a dozen different businesses, each one different to the last. First he "specialised" in clearing credit card debt; then he was peddling utilities and mobile phones; next he's facilitating no win no fee court cases - you know, "that guy".

In early 2011 it seemed like he'd stopped messing around and had settled on something which made a bit more sense and could have been a viable business - he was promoting himself as a networking coach. Putting aside the complete lack of credibility he had as a legit business person, he did have a lot of networking experience, and so this was something he could have run with. It seemed others agreed, and the negative sentiment within the network turned positive; he even got involved in setting up groups for that network within his region, putting him in a position of solid visibility and influence. While I've always had distaste for this person, even I started to come round.

Then out of the blue, he left the network to get involved with a different networking group, one with greater financial incentives for people running the show. Shocker.

6 months on and he's changed lanes again, now he's a property investor, apparently, and he's back in his original networking group, albeit with his credibility back to zero. Had he just recognised that after years of trying he'd finally found something which could work and stuck with it, he'd be able to stop the constant scrambling and clutching for ways to make money, and would avoid diluting his personal marketing message to a point where it's difficult for anyone to take him seriously.

I'm sure we've all encountered a plethora of people like that over the years, but it doesn't just apply to small businesses - take Pizza Hut for example. You'd be hard pressed to find anyone who hasn't heard of Pizza Hut, or who can't tell you what it is they do (for anyone struggling, the clue is in the name...). Pizza Hut have found themselves struggling a little bit recently in light of more contenders to the fast food restaurant industry entering the fray, along with their main rivals Dominos dominating the takeaway market. However in a true "WTF" move, rather than focus on improving or better promoting their core offering, they changed it.

Yep, Pizza Hut took a whole bunch of their restaurants and took Pizza off the menu. Crazy, right? Renaming those restaurants "Pasta Hut" didn't do them any favours, and for a prolonged period of time there was an air of confusion about whether your local restaurant was still doing pizza or not; or indeed whether Pizza Hut as a company were going to stop doing pizzas altogether. Not a great position to be in when you're already slipping in the market!

Fortunately they seem to have done a u-turn and Pasta Hut is a thing of the past(-a); however even now it seems they're almost embarrassed by the fact they serve pizza, their latest TV ad focusing almost entirely on salad, though I may have glimpsed a split second shot of a Meat Feast.

In this ever changing world you have to keep moving and stay active within your business, particularly when it comes to marketing - however moving in a completely different direction can cause a lot of damage if not thought through properly or done for the right reasons.

Don't build a shop, build a high street

28

Do you offer everything your customers may need? I'm not talking about selling your customers groceries while you fix their computer, but if you're fixing their computer do you also have the ability to sell them new parts? Software? Accessories? What about training on how to use it? Remote support? Do you build computers and sell them yourself? Can you help to arrange Internet access for them? And if so can you sort out their telephone line too?

Chances are you don't do all of that, or whatever the equivalent mish-mash of products and services would be for your industry. If not, then what you have is a shop, when what your customer needs is to be on a high street. You can't avoid that, but what you could do is make sure all of the shops on that high street are owned by you!

Before you rush off and put down a deposit on half of your local city centre, I am of course talking figuratively. Let me give you an example:

My other half (most say better half!) Callie Willows is a wonderfully talented person. She's a nutritional therapist, naturopath and homeopath, and despite being wicked smart and having a particular gift for marketing she was having trouble with turning these skills into a viable and profitable business model.

Initially she was dealing almost solely with client consultations, however as with any business which revolves around a sole practitioner this brought with it a raft of limitations. Last year she set in motion a range of projects, products and different services which all fall into her areas of expertise.

Now in addition to working with clients directly, she also has a number of e-commerce sites selling supplements and vitamins, a series of books about dietary challenges, as well online training courses and informational sites.

Previously when she was conducting health tests on her clients, her reports included a number of suggestions and recommendations regarding lifestyle and diet; however I'm sure we'd all admit to being a little lax when it comes to our health, and so she often found herself frustrated when clients didn't take recommended actions.

Now, however, when she recommends a change in diet, she has her own books which she can direct them to. When she suggests a lifestyle switch or a change in mindset there are courses and information available which she can send them to. If they need to take a particular vitamin or supplement she owns the store they can buy them from. If they find out they have a condition or are prone to stress etc then she offers a monthly subscription service with set packs of supplements sent by post every month (www.healthinabox.net - check it out!).

Instead of just taking it on the chin that clients weren't following up, or allowing herself to fall into the trap of constantly working in the business rather than on it, and having her success limited by this approach - she looked at where her clients would or should go after she's "done" with them, and made sure she set up her stall there too. As all of these ventures fall within the remit of her expertise then she doesn't suffer from giving off a negative "jack of all trades" message, and not only is she able to boost her own success but she has the satisfaction of enabling clients to follow up on her advice and actually make a positive change in their lives.

What else do your clients need? Where do they go to before and after they've been to you? Can you provide what they need without appearing opportunist? Make sure your stall is set out right up that high street, otherwise other people will take up that space and will get your customers business.

Who are your competitors, really?

29

While attitudes towards competition are slowly changing for the better and towards looking for collaborative opportunities, most business owners still keep an eye firmly fixed on what their competitors are up to. That is, of course, a smart thing to do - it's healthy and strategically sound to know what others in your industry are doing (so long as you don't become obsessed!). However, most people are somewhat short-sighted when it comes to determining just who their competition is.

So who are your competitors, *really?*

Of course others who swim in the same pond as you and offer the same products or services are your direct competition, but you need to look a little deeper than that. If you run a restaurant, what function are you providing to people? If you made a quick list you may come up with the following:

- Somewhere to eat
- Somewhere to eat Italian food
- Somewhere to go on special occasions
- Somewhere to take a date
- Somewhere local to go to pass time

Most people would focus on the first two, and as such would look at other businesses nearby who serve food, specifically Italian food, and designate them as their competition, without looking any further. However, the true competition lies with anything else which fulfils the other needs on that list.

So if a new cinema opens up nearby, that could become the place people start going to pass time when they want to get out and do something. If the local council make improvements to a nearby park then you may lose customers who prefer to take their dates for a romantic stroll instead of a Carbonara; and if the local bowling alley introduces new group rates then you could lose people who typically come to your place for parties.

Delving a bit further into identifying your true competition isn't rocket science; it just may not be the most obvious thing to do as the "immediate" competitors will be numerous to the point you mightn't actually want to look further for fear of putting yourself off running a business!

I'd urge you, however, to take the extra time to look further into whom or what could challenge you for your customers' money, time and attention.

White label what you do

30

I'm a massive fan of white-labelling stuff, the concept of facilitating someone else's ability to sell your services under their own brand. This materialises in all shapes and sizes. Most web companies (me included) offer web hosting for their customers which is provided by a larger hosting company and supplied on a white label basis. So you see my name and logo throughout your hosting control panel and my name appears on the direct debit etc. I manage and maintain everything, but the server space is provided by someone else with the infrastructure and experience to help me to provide a great service,

Many products, or services which have been packaged as products, lend themselves very well to white labelling, particularly software; but it's entirely possible to white label yourself as a service provider too.

A number of professions feature freelancers, who by their nature are there to "plug in" to another company when needed; however the smart ones will make themselves more attractive to hire by, say, providing a white label version of the documents they use in their day to day work - questionnaires, client reports etc - the sort of deliverables you would want to give to your client, provided to you with space for you to put your logo on them.

A graphic designer I know by the name of Gareth Coxon of Dot Design (www.dot-design.co.uk) does this brilliantly. He has a completely editable client questionnaire which I can pop my logo on and send to a potential customer who needs something I don't provide; he has fixed price packages with room for me to make a little bit of profit; and he is more than willing to attend meetings under the banner of another company.

Matt Purser, a friend of mine who also runs a web design company called Edgeward (www.edgeward.co.uk) - has nearly a dozen business cards from other companies with his name on who use him as their "in- house" web guy because he offers a white-label proposition where he will interact with the clients and attend meetings as Matt from x, y or z as and when needed.

While it is, of course, important to invest in and protect your own brand, you shouldn't be too precious about it if there's the potential to white label yourself, your products and your services in a manner which benefits you, your potential collaborators, and their clients; and when in that sort of relationship there are so many quick wins as simple as providing unbranded documents which help to grease those wheels so much more effectively.

What problem do you solve?

31

When crafting their marketing message, many people focus so much on blowing their own trumpet and explaining how great their products are that they forget about what's important - the customers.

People aren't going to buy something on the basis of how good you tell them you are. There has to be a want or a need which exists for the customer - you need to solve a problem. That problem can be as superficial as their need to "keep up with the joneses" by having the latest stuff, or it may be a real issue such as a health problem or a financial issue.

Basic sales training encourages you to sell the benefits above the features, but again many people to wrong by interpreting the benefits as they see them, rather than how their customers will realistically see them.

You need to identify, at a raw, basic level, what problem you solve. Do you enable people to do things quicker? Are you cheaper while offering the same value? Do you make their lives easier, more fulfilling? Can you play on discomfort? Tap in to insecurities?

In general people tend to have a greater urge to run away from things rather than run to them - so if something about your products or services enables you to solve an issue which may be troubling your customer then you need to put this front and centre. That's why affiliate marketers (people who make a living promoting other peoples products) tend to make a lot more money from weight loss products, aides for quitting smoking, and - no surprises - erectile dysfunction treatments.

This is also why a lot of successful campaigns for products which don't necessarily solve the sort of problems outlined above tend to focus on manipulating the fear of missing out on a special offer.

Your product or service must serve some sort of purpose and as such must solve some sort of problem and plug some gap for your customers - so put this at the heart of your marketing message rather than focusing on congratulating yourself.

Go niche

32

Back in the dreaded days of employment I was invited to a networking event by a local firm of accountants, and as I ended up joining that networking organisation I ended up seeing a lot of them. Over time we developed a great relationship, and being employed at the time I got them in to take over accountancy duties at the company I worked for.

That company specialised in helping start-up businesses, and so we were perfectly positioned to make referrals to this accountancy firm, which we did in abundance. When I decided to break free of my employed shackles, I turned to these guys first, and it was a no brainer that I'd use them as my own accountants.

Over a period of 18 months I developed a fantastic relationship with these guys, both business and personal, so when they decided they wanted a new website they came to me. We had a chat, I provided a quote, and they promised to call when they were ready to proceed.

That call never came.

A month or so later when I saw them again, I gently nudged them about where we were with regards their website. They told me, rather awkwardly, that they'd decided to go with another company. I'll admit I was a bit peeved, ordinarily if a potential client decides to go another route I don't take it personally as it's down to them to decide what is best for their business; however because of my relationship with these guys I was determined to find out why.

The company they chose weren't local, weren't clients of theirs, in fact they didn't know anybody there. They hadn't been referred or recommended, and price-wise they were comparable. The reason they chose them over me?

They specialise solely in websites for accountants.

The moral to that lengthy preamble? Having a niche is a bloody powerful thing. So powerful that it superseded extremely long and strong relationships.

The funny thing is that the company they chose did exactly the same as I would have, their work was of a similar quality, they coded in the same language, and the features of the finished website were the same ones I'd discussed building; however by being savvy, picking a single niche, and building their entire brand, message and proposition around it they were able to torpedo any other "generalist" company.

There's a well known phrase in marketing of "sell the sizzle, not the sausage" - in this instance we were selling identical sausages; they'd just engineered their "sizzle" to a specific market. Oftentimes that is the only difference between a company with a general, cover-all offering and one with a niche proposition - the packaging!

A graphic designer who specialises in the motor trade is still offering graphic design services; the sales workshop a trainer delivers to a group of estate agents most likely has been adapted from general sales tips, and so on.

A big difference maker, of course, is credibility and experience in a certain field. Of all the industries I've worked with, I've worked with estate agents and recruitment companies the most, and the closest, which has enabled me to offer specific products and services to those two industries.

There may be something similar for you, or perhaps your education or work experience is in a certain field. If you have experience in one particular industry in your arsenal, and offer a product or service which could easily be adapted to a niche, then this puts you in a powerful position indeed.

The question is, however, do you want to have a niche business or a generalist one? Well, with a bit of clever marketing, branding and structuring there's no reason why you can't do both! Whether that's two separate companies, or simply segregating your branding, it's up to you! For me this takes the form of two separate products, each with their own name, logo, brand, web presence etc; completely independent of my other ventures. As they are products, this then does not make it difficult to mention them where appropriate to customers of my main businesses in the same way I might recommend Wordpress for blogging or Magento for ecommerce.

Similarly as they have their own self-contained brand, customers buy those products directly and associate that brand with their specific industry.

So if there's a particular area you like working in, expertise which is going untapped, or an industry you have extensive experience in, why not take a look at your current offering and see whether it's feasible to take the niche route, as it's an extremely potent path to take.

Keep your ears to the ground

33

I'm sure the majority of you will know of or had experience with Business Link, the government backed organisation responsible for providing support and advice to businesses of all shapes and sizes. While there's no doubt that they had a positive influence on a great number of people, they were always dogged with people bemoaning various aspects of their service, in particular how much it cost to keep them running.

When it was announced in 2011 that the service would be shut down there was a great deal of speculation as to what would fill the gap, and so interest was high when the "Start-up Britain" initiative was launched.

Start-up Britain was a collective effort by a number of large, high profile businesses and individuals, and was derided by a large number of people for being generic, not useful, and for suffering from nepotism by largely promoting services provided by its founders. There was particular criticism from the creative industries due to the promotion of a US service which is widely considered by those in the industry to be harmful to the design community.

There was, of course, some positive feedback, but by and large reaction across blogs and social media was mostly negative. While people were busy complaining, however, some were being quite shrewd and capitalising on the furore to launch their own alternatives to what Start-up Britain was offering.

By keeping their ears to the ground they were able to gauge the main concerns, and release products and services to counter them.

A friend of mine, Lee Rickler who runs Point and Stare (www.pointandstare.com), a web development agency in London, brought out his own start-up Britain web packages, with features and special pricing aimed specifically at start-ups, and angled so as to provide a strong alternative.

Lee was able to tap in to the ongoing conversations about the service and use them as a basis to discuss and promote his own offerings. Now as far as I know Lee wasn't offering anything different to what he normally did; he just packaged and promoted it in direct relation to a hot topic amongst small business owners and start-ups.

The chatter about Start-up Britain has long since simmered down, but whenever the topic rears its head again Lee has this card up his sleeve.

This is just a small example of the benefit of keeping your ears to the ground for hot topics of discussion amongst your market. Check out forums, keep an eye on social networks, listen to what your market are talking about and find a way to put yourself and your products into that conversation

Who ruins your industry?

34

Everyone I talk to in business always has a story about someone in their industry - a company, individual, or a particular "type" of practitioner - who gives it a bad name. Often this is used as an excuse for things being difficult - "nobody trusts financial advisors because of blah blah", "it's hard to sell quality websites because people would rather buy cheap rubbish from such-and-such.com".

Instead of bemoaning these people, you should really be embracing them, because they either set the bar low enough for you to vault over, or provide a basis for comparison in order for you to demonstrate just why you are the better alternative.

If there are elements of your industry which you're not happy about, position yourself as the polar opposite, and don't be afraid to take a stand and speak your mind. Blogging is great for this - you do, of course, have to be careful how you do it otherwise you could come across as whiny or jealous; or if you start naming names could land yourself in serious trouble!

4Networking, who I've mentioned a few times, are a great example of this. Their MD, Brad Burton, looked at everything which he considered bad about business networking, and formulated his offering around providing an alternative; centring their marketing around the fact that unlike many of the main national networking groups, his was unstuffy and unencumbered with the rules, pomp and ceremony typically found elsewhere.

Don't be afraid to go against the norm, or to be "anti-industry". Website design is an industry typically viewed by the average business owner as one to be wary of due to the vast number of cowboys, and the ease with which you can end up being ripped off. Ask any good web geek about the less savoury elements of this unregulated industry and you'll find they soon fire off into a huge rant. I'm exactly the same, and have actually structured a lot of my marketing around it, much of it taking the form of videos which can be found on AngryGeek.biz.

For me, speaking my mind and speaking against the elements which ruin my industry has enabled me to be seen as a "champion of regular business folk" amongst some circles when it comes web "stuff", something which has been massively beneficial and is exceptionally difficult to achieve by any other means.

ASSUME THE POSITION

84

Your message

Every business has a voice; and if you're a one-man band, or running a small business, then that voice is yours! But honing your message is not just about what you say; it's about what you do, how you conduct yourself, and the impression you leave on everyone you interact with.

Business, and the world of small business in particular, has seen a lot of the formality stripped away from it over the last 5-10 years. The suited and booted car salesman of old is becoming a relic of how business used to be done, and some of the most successful business people in the world are today turning up to work in flip-flops and a hoodie.

People simply aren't as impressed by the overblown hype, fancy suits and expensive cars as they used to be. Baffling people with science or manipulating people into buying from you are no longer easy ways of scoring a quick sale. Authenticity and simplicity are the key to effectively reaching your market, so your message needs to hit those marks.

This is good news for small businesses – because unless you're a budding criminal mastermind, chances are that you can truly be authentic. Furthermore in the past we've all no doubt struggled with the best way to make what we do sound more than it actually is – not to mislead people, but to try to use flowery language to demonstrate the worth and substance of what we're selling. And so a move towards more simplistic, plain-English communication saves us a lot of that hassle.

All of this makes it far easier to get your message right – however doing so often means unlearning a lot of the bad habits which have somehow been accepted as "how it's done" – so let's start that process now...

Don't patronise, empathise

This one stems from a personal bugbear of mine, but is definitely something worth keeping in mind. A guy who used to regularly attend the same networking meetings as I did used to deliver the same "elevator" speech which, every time I heard it, had me cringing in my seat.

This guy was a business coach, and would frequently make reference to his ability to help small businesses "down here" (try to imagine him holding his hand at waist height), get to "up here" (as he emphatically thrust his hand above his head).

It wasn't so much the sentiment, but the tone and phrasing he used as he spoke down with particular venom to small business owners, the very people sitting in the same room as him. Needless to say I never once came across a single person who had opted to use his services from within that networking crowd (or anywhere else for that matter!).

What made it worse, or more laughable depending on how you look at it, is that he wasn't from some huge company, nor was he a notable business person himself; he was "just another small business" with the same issues and struggles as everyone else.

Had he taken an approach of empathy rather than patronising people, then people will undoubtedly have warmed to him. Very few people have an all-encompassing toolkit, so all this guy needed to do was to talk about that and tell people what he could bring to their table. A little bit of honesty goes a long way - nobody would judge him negatively if, for example, he highlighted the fact that he doesn't know how to build a website or do accounts and so it makes sense for him to work with people who do - so by extension people who couldn't do what he does would be well served working with him etc.

As it stood, he was seen as abrasive and, as one fellow networker described him, a "delusional business snob". All he had to do was change his tact (and his attitude!) slightly and he could have been on to a winner.

I experience this sort of person frequently in the web design industry - people who will jump on any opportunity to run down clients and throw snide comments at them for having a poor website. The most successful web designers I know who deal with small businesses do well because they understand that people starting a business don't have thousands of pounds, typically, to throw at a site; and so they try to work with those people rather than make them feel stupid or inadequate.

It makes far more sense to position yourself on your potential clients' side rather than taking an adversarial position - if you have to bully and patronise people into a sale it doesn't bode well for a long and fruitful relationship.

Hold back on the hype

36

Guru, genius, serial entrepreneur, expert.

Vomit.

It might just be me but I absolutely hate these words, especially when they're part of a self- proclamation! Personally I feel that it's down to other people to call you an expert, you don't just declare yourself to be one.

There are some people who can pull it off, where calling themselves a genius fits their persona, and where you know they genuinely don't consider themselves Mensa material. For these people it works because of who they are and the character they have, and it's a great way of drawing attention to their achievements.

Brad Burton is an example of this - his personal brand strap line is "Author, Speaker, Genius" - with the genius part relating to what some people referred to his success with 4Networking being. This works for Brad because of his raw, over the top persona. The downside of this, however, is that within weeks of Brad adopting this strap line, about a dozen or so other people completely devoid of Brad's charisma started touting themselves as geniuses too. For these people it simply did not work, and actually made them look a little pompous and silly!

"Guru" is the more commonly used one these days, particularly when it comes to Social Media. I have no idea where the trend came from but it has quickly become one of my biggest bugbears and tends to garner overwhelmingly negative reactions from anyone with more than a couple of brain cells.

Often it's because the people referring to themselves as "gurus" have nothing to back it up, and more often than not they are the bandwagon jumpers who give their industry a bad name.

The last one for me is "serial entrepreneur" - again, a label people bandy around to big themselves up. To me, however, that just says you have failed numerous times!

I'd best stop there as this runs the risk of becoming one big rant, but the point is that over-hyping yourself can be very dangerous and can backfire and achieve the complete opposite result than that you were looking for. Calling yourself an expert, guru or genius simply puts you under greater scrutiny and if you're found to not live up to your own inflated labels then you'll be laughed at.

Trust me, I'm an expert.

I vs. We

37

This is a debate which I've seen rage across a variety of business forums over the years, and is one which I've tended to avoid simply because I've always been torn. It's the question of whether a one-man band should refer to themselves and their business as "I" or "We" in their website copy, promotional material, and when talking to others about their business.

Saying "we do xyz" can make a one man band seem larger than they are and by extension more legit, stable and worthy of doing business with. This is both the argument for (if you're the one man band in question) and the argument against (if you're an outside observer with a bee in their bonnet) - in that it can be argued that saying "we" instead of "I" could be seen as misrepresenting yourself.

Unless you're positioned as a freelancer, or promoting something entirely based around your personal brand, then saying "I" can be an uncomfortable thing, and for a lot of people, "we" naturally comes out (avoiding the obvious juvenile joke here) when writing or talking about their business.

Personally, I use "we", even though I am a one man band. However while I don't employ anyone directly in my business, I collaborate with and outsource to other web geeks and creatives, I use a virtual assistant to handle my admin, a call answering service to manage my calls, an accountant to add stuff up, business mentors and other advisors. As such I view my businesses as a collective effort - saying "I" simply doesn't represent all of that, and while I never lie about having employees, I do feel comfortable referring to my company as "we", because all of those people I involve in my business are vital pieces of the puzzle.

The key to all of this, in my view, is that you need to make a decision on which you're going to use, and stick with it. Worse than using "I" or "we" incorrectly is using both of them inconsistently. As long as you're confident in how you're crafting your message, consistent in doing it, and can justify/explain your choice of wording if challenged then you're set.

It really comes down to positioning. Are you a person, or are you representing a company? Using "we" over "I" creates distance between the person writing/speaking and the subject they're discussing. It's the same reason why we have the "royal we", as well as the "editorial we" employed by journalists to separate their opinions from that of the publication.

There will still be those who strongly believe that "we" is reserved for companies with more than one employee/director, however if the issue is ensuring accurate representation of your business then surely the whole idea of using a company name or brand for a one man band is flawed too. If we must all refer to ourselves as "I" then surely every one person enterprise should carry the name of its proprietor. However what then happens when that business does take on an employee - do they change their company name? Do they have to revise all of their website content and redesign all of their promotional material? It simply doesn't make sense.

You can, of course, avoid the issue completely by staying clear of pro-nouns, replacing "I" or "we" with the name of your company. It won't necessarily flow well, and will definitely sound a bit awkward, however at least you'll avoid this contentious issue!

Mixed motives

38

This one really did make me chuckle...

There was an article in the press a few months ago detailing the worst speed camera in the UK. The reason it was the "worst" was because it had generated the lowest revenues of all the active speed cameras across the country.

Amusing considering that as they were being introduced, and to this day, speed cameras are marketed to us as being there to make our roads safer, reduce traffic speeds and as a result help to prevent accidents.

Presumably a camera which generated the least revenue did so because people driving past it were going below the speed limit... Which means it's achieving what - we're told - is its purpose; surely this makes it the UK's best speed camera, not the worst!

Thankfully we're not naive enough to think that road safety is the reason for these ghastly things; we all know they're just big yellow cash points for local authorities - but if you're going to sell it to "us" on the basis of its safety implications then something like this article revealing the true motives is a major faux pas.

So the lesson learned is that if you need to disguise your true motives through marketing, you really need to make sure you don't trip up like these prats did!

Appearance is nothing

39

This is a talking point which rears its head with frustrating regularity - the debate over whether what you wear, what you drive etc are indicators of whether someone should do business with you.

There is still a huge chunk of the business community, at both ends of the scale, who will look down on anyone not driving the latest Audi whatever-series (cars aren't my forte as you may tell!); and that's not an attitude that will be shifted easily.

Personally I think this whole mindset is backwards and outdated, but recognise that this snobbery does exist and so is something to be mindful of. Whether you play along and rack up huge dry cleaning and car lease bills is entirely up to you - if you feel more comfortable playing dress-up "successful business owner", or are in an industry where these antiquated mindsets are far to prevalent to overcome then go for it, polish the cuff links and iron your tie!

I've held off on the flash cars because, frankly, I can't be trusted in one. I've had so many daft mishaps in the short time I've been driving (only got round to taking my test a few years ago) that it's almost guaranteed I'd bugger up an expensive car the second it was off the forecourt.

Personally I don't care one bit what people think of my rather modest (and unwashed) 05 Focus - I'm in the nice comfortable position where I can pick and choose the clients I work with and if my car makes a difference to you, then you're not going to like the bloke who drives it either - and chances are if you're that stuffy I'm really not going to like you!

It's the same reason I don't really censor my tweets, forum posts etc as much as others would caution you to - I don't have the time nor inclination to maintain any sort of facade, so if you do business with me because I act well spoken and drive a fancy car you'd end up getting a nasty shock when the veneer drops and a sweary Geordie troglodyte appears.

Ultimately for me, the only thing that wearing a fancy suit proves is that you know where to buy a suit; and if you're a small business owner driving a flash car I'm assuming you've lumbered yourself with a loan or pricey lease plan in order to afford it. None of this stuff is any indication of your ability to do the job.

The caveat to this – however – is the idea of "eating your own dog food". If your business is about creating wealth for others, then a beat-up mini might not instil confidence; in the same way as an overweight personal trainer is unlikely to inspire people to work with them. In these sorts of instances then a little more consideration to appearance is warranted; however there's no reason why a graphic designer or a plumber needs to turn up to meetings in a three-piece suit!

Lies, damn lies, and statistics

40

Something which has occurred to me recently is that I'm really not very good at lying. I don't have the sort of memory and attention span to keep up any pretence, and I tend to overcompensate, spinning a yarn so convoluted and complex that it very quickly tangles around me and trips me up.

So when it comes to promoting and representing myself and my business I find the much easier option is just to be honest and straightforward; something which others I do business with tend to do too.

However I have, as I'm sure you have too, encountered a number of people who are - bluntly - full of it.

One particular person comes to mind for me. I'm not going to name names; though I know several people reading this who know me and networked in the same circles will know exactly who I'm talking about - so famed was this person for his outlandish BS.

I don't condone or suggest lying to people while marketing your business, but if you absolutely must, then for the love of god figure out how to lie well!

The guy who epitomises this point for me was a sales coach. He would frequently boast of increasing Mr. Client-of-the-weeks turnover by 2003% (never a round number, because people might suspect something) from a single sales coaching session with him. Problem is that most of the time one of us would know who he was talking about, and on getting the full story it was either a massive exaggeration, or creativity with the before and after figures, or taking credit for sales which would already have come in with or without this guys input.

The biggest string to this persons bow was that he did a 6 figure sales deal with a well known celebrity - since deceased. His website was adorned with a huge photo of him shaking hands with this personality, complete with a snippet from a recommendation letter written after their "deal". Such was the profile of this deal that this guy had written a book specifically about working with this celeb, and had embarked on a speaking tour, talking about nothing but how he sold to such a big name.

As it turned out, this huge deal was actually a small print order; the letter of recommendation was actually something this guy had begged for under the guise of needing it for a job application, and the hand-shaking photograph was taken at a public event for this personality's charity. All of this came out when the family of this high-profile figure were alerted to this guys activity by people who had been ripped off by him, and in a move which made the major local press they swiftly ordered him to remove all references and stop all activity falsely trading on their lost loved ones name which, knowing he'd been rumbled, he quickly complied with.

He went silent for a couple of months, tried to drop off the radar of people who knew him and what he'd been up to, but I've heard tales of him peddling the same rubbish around.

Daft thing is that if he just tempered his exaggeration and lied "well", he'd not only be taken more seriously but also wouldn't have seen his reputation implode and a massive chunk of his potential market disappear.

This isn't an isolated incident though - you don't have to go far to find an internet marketing "expert" peddling a £10 eBook or downloadable course promising the secrets of how they make £20,000 a day for only an hour's work. Seriously...
If these people were smart, they'd be selling the secrets to making £500

a day for 4 hours of work, which is a hell of a lot more feasible. Of course the big figures appeal to the, let's face it, stupid people - but taking a more feasible approach would actually draw in the smarter people too. Hell, I'd take a £10 punt on something like that because it's something I could have a realistic expectation of living up to its grounded and very possible promise.

So if you're going to exaggerate, don't go so over the top that what you're saying becomes unrealistic because most people aren't stupid; and if you absolutely must lie, lie well!

Make your offering memorable & shareable

41

One of the most useful things about using business networking as part of your marketing strategy is that most organisations encourage or require you to summarise your business proposition in less than 60 seconds.

Obviously the main reason for this is for time keeping purposes at these events, but it's something which is also a fantastic exercise which can reap dividends elsewhere in your business.

A lot of us in small business took this path because we have a particular skill which we are very knowledgeable and passionate about, and so when asked what we do we often end up rambling. Same goes for companies who offer a selection of products or services - when faced with giving a 60 second "elevator speech" they try to cram in a list of everything they do.

Such time constraints make even the best marketing and sales people forget the basics, and so they rattle off a laundry list of "features" of what they do, rather than keeping it simple, covering just one or two core benefits, and making their offering memorable and shareable.

If you can sum up what you can do for me, in under 60 seconds, then even if I don't have a need for what you do right now, I can associate that simple sound bite with you and your business, and store it away in my mental "Rolodex". Not only does this make it easy for me to choose you when I have a need for your product or service, but it makes it really easy for me to tell others what you do too.

The same applies to other marketing methods - within seconds of picking up your brochure, flyer, or visiting your website I should have a solid idea of what it is you do. If I want to find out more and drill into the specifics, then I'll do so, but you can't rely on everyone wanting to go that step further, or having the patience to try to figure out what it is you offer.

So make sure your offering is simple, memorable and shareable; otherwise people won't understand, remember or share it!

Dealing with people

People are strange, and as an anti-social geek at heart I'm perhaps the last person you'd expect (or want) to tell you how best to deal with them! However while I'm not likely to turn you into a social animal, I can give you advice on the "people part" of your marketing strategy.

Unless you've managed to get your dog approved for a credit card, it's a fair bet to say that other people play a role in almost every element of operating your business – and so you need to make sure you cater towards them as effectively as possible.

People can be the greatest asset of any business, but also a destructive force if you get things wrong – even more so with the rise of social media giving a global voice to anyone with a grievance to air.

Don't make the mistake of thinking that the only people who matter are those who line your pockets. Suppliers, supporters, advocates and fans can boost your business in a way money can't buy; and while this is perhaps a little too much like clichéd sales patter, everyone is a potential customer.

We have a distinct advantage in this area, however – in that we are people too! It's amazing how some forget this, or neglect to put themselves into other people's shoes when considering their customer service or their sales and marketing strategy.

Of course you want to avoid meticulously analysing every person you come into contact with – but if you can get to grips with the basics of what people want, what annoys them, what appeals to them etc, then you can be well on your way to using that knowledge to your advantage when it comes to marketing your business.

The way to a client's heart

42

People love free. People love food. People go absolutely crazy for free food!

I once attended an exhibition where a company run by an acquaintance of mine had taken a stand. This was their first exhibition and they were determined to make an impact so spent an absolute fortune on promotional materials, high end display stands, fantastic matching branded t-shirts, standees with 24inch LCD screens showing a looping video for which they'd hired professional film crews... the works.

They got visitors, and some enquiries, but nowhere near as many as the company a few stalls down, who offered a similar set of services. They had a plain table, with some home printed leaflets, cut to shape by the business owner with a pair of what must have been pretty blunt scissors, and the guy manning the stand was stuffed awkwardly into an ill-fitting suit that closely resembled one I'd seen in the sales at Asda. His table, however, was overrun with visitors, for the entire day, and a sneak peek revealed that his clipboard for taking down enquiries was onto its third full sheet of A4.

The difference? Chocolate Hob Nobs.

This guy had boxes upon boxes of them, and most of his table space was taken up with plates covered in biscuits, which he kept restocked throughout the day.

Sure, there were a huge amount of drive-by biscuit snatchers who would feign interest just as an excuse to grab three biscuits (not guilty... I only grabbed 2 the second time...), but those who weren't quite so flagrant would stop for a chat, and these chats were leading into genuine enquiries.

My friend spent close to £4000 on material for this exhibition. This guy most likely spent around £30 on biscuits.

Sticking with the biscuit theme, a guy I network with called Tom Lawrence runs a stationery company (www.tlcoffice-supplies.co.uk) - he hands out free Kit Kat's at every networking meeting, and all customers get free biscuits sent with every order. I was exchanging a few comments with him about this on twitter one evening, and at the end of the conversation I put in an order for a flip chart. I didn't really need the flip chart, it was something which was always on the "nice to have, but not really needed" list. I was convinced to order, however, by the free tin of Victoria biscuits I was told would accompany it. No word of a lie.

Never underestimate the power of free food!

Your customer is always right?

43

This saying has always grated on me. In my first job in telesales when I was 16, I firmly believed that no matter what, anything the customer said was right, regardless of whether I knew it wasn't. This carried through to every job I worked, and was the cornerstone of dozens of customer service training sessions I attended and then, later, wrote and delivered to the latest bunch of saps!

It is, of course, utter nonsense. The sentiment of keeping your customer happy seems to have become lost amidst this bizarre prescriptive notion that standing up to a customer or fighting your corner is an absolute no-no.

Don't get me wrong, a lot of the time the customers happiness needs to trump your own in order to maintain a harmonious relationship - but that doesn't mean you need to let them walk all over you.

An extreme example happened to me recently. A company who subcontracts to me won a piece of work to salvage a website for a major florist. We managed to "save the day" and get their website up and running in time for a big event they had planned. However, once the panic was over they started asking for a whole bunch of stuff which was outside of the agreement, and throwing some ludicrous timescales at us.

We agreed to take on the extra work, even though it meant a hard slog over a tight timeframe, and very quickly I found myself being bombarded with emails and phone calls from their marketing manager. One Saturday while lying in bed I heard my phone vibrating in the other room. As it was 11.30pm I left it.

A minute later it started vibrating again... Then again, then again a few minutes after that. Fully awake and slightly annoyed I went to check who was calling me, and found that I had 6 missed calls, 4 text messages and 8 emails, all from this florists marketing manager. There was no emergency, she was just irate that I hadn't returned her first call (at 11.30pm) so proceeded to keep calling over and over, accompanied by increasingly abusive texts and emails.

Normally I'm quite laid back, but this was a bit too much, and knowing it wouldn't stop till I spoke to her, I called her back. What followed was not the highlight of my career, as I found myself embroiled in an extremely heated and very loud argument over the phone, with a client. She felt that it was wholly unacceptable for me to be "ignoring" her calls that night, to which I actually screamed at her about how ridiculous it was to expect her calls to be answered at 11.30 on a Saturday night. This went on for about half an hour...

Now I've said this wasn't my proudest moment, and in my entire career I've rarely so much as raised my voice slightly to a client - the majority of whom I quickly develop a great deal of affection for - however this was just a bit too much to take!

I'm not condoning arguing with clients like this, but the end result was a much greater level of mutual respect and a stronger and more fluid working relationship. We get along fantastically now and I've been promised to be lavished with food and alcohol next time I venture into London.

That is definitely a more extreme example and is not something I would hope to never repeat for the rest of my career - but the alternative? To have a client view me as a complete pushover who they could order around at any crazy hour they pleased? That's a message you need to nip in the bud.

So of course, keep your clients happy, but not at all costs; and certainly not by doing things which completely undermine you and your business.

Build a bridge
by Tamsen Garrie

44

We've all had that experience where we've just 'clicked' instantly with someone: the connection is instant, the conversation flows easily and effortlessly and there's that feeling of you both being on the same wavelength. Well, that's rapport in action!
Rapport is crucial in business and particularly in the context of sales and referrals. People buy from people and so whilst having a desirable product or service and the ability to explain why it's so great is imperative, so is the ability to sell you!

What is rapport?

Rapport is a relationship of mutual understanding and/or trust. I like to think of rapport like a bridge - the stronger the bridge, the more it can hold. What I mean by that is the stronger the rapport you have with someone, the more you can expect from the relationship. The stronger the rapport, the more chance you have of finding out what the other person needs from you and the more likely you are to receive what you need from them.

Whilst the subject of rapport is vast, fundamentally, there are two very simply principles:

One: People like people who they think are like them
Two: People like people who they think like them

When someone thinks that we are like them (commonality) or that we like them, it's hard for them not to like us back.

So, how can you make it easy for people to see that you are like them, or that you like them?

You need to apply the one simple rule of rapport: Be as much like the other person as you can be.

This doesn't mean changing who you are, or 'mimicking' the other person. It simply means adapting your natural style of communication to the extent that it is still comfortable and authentic for you, but so that it also 'meets' the other person. This is otherwise known as Adaptability: The ability to adapt our approach to the person or situation with which we are dealing. What tends to happen when we apply adaptability is that the other person naturally and subconsciously meets us back.

How does this relate specifically to sales?

If you know someone who is exceptional at sales, I can guarantee you that they are applying adaptability (whether they are consciously aware of it or not).

Adaptability means talking to people in a way that makes it easy for them to listen to you and in the context of sales, selling to people the way they're comfortable buying (as opposed to the way that you are comfortable selling!)

Be honest - when was the last time you were in a sales situation and your potential client/customer said to you "this is how I like to buy"? Most people will not 'tell' you how they like to buy, but they will 'show' you. Often, we are so intent on getting others to see our own point of view that we don't notice the other person and the signals they give us.

So, next time you are in a sales situation, take some time to observe the other person and notice the verbal (what they say), vocal (How they say it) and visual (what they do when they say it) signals they give you. How do they talk? What language do they use? How do they sit or move?

When you observe the other person rather than fixating on your own agenda, you are then able to adapt your own behaviour to that which is conducive to establishing rapport.

Demonstrate Interest. Ask questions and then ensure that you listen to the answer. There is nothing more off-putting than the knowledge that the other person is not listening to you.

Demonstrate understanding. Nod, and perhaps even repeat what they have said in your own words (paraphrase) to show that you have understood. If you don't understand, ask questions and listen until you do.

Demonstrate empathy. What they are saying may not be important to you, but so what? If it's important to them and you empathise with them, you'll create rapport.

Demonstrate Commonality. We are instinctively connected with people with whom we share things in common. If someone like golf and so do you – talk with them about it.

Rapport is key to life and business and particularly to sales. Those with whom you build rapport may become your clients/customers and if they don't, they will at least become your advocates, referring clients/customers your way.

Tamsen Garrie runs Alpha Associates, specialising in business strategy and skills training.
www.alpha-associates.biz
www.tamwithaplan.co.uk

Encourage feedback

45

One of the hardest things for the corporate world to get to grips with amidst the rise of social media is the notion that they are no longer in control of their message. People are out there, they're talking about products and services, and the people behind those products and services have no way of controlling what is being said.

This is undoubtedly the main reason why a lot of the "big boys" were so slow to adopt social media, why many still haven't, and why a lot of those who have are using completely the wrong approach.

While on the face of it this fear is understandable, when you think beyond the horror of people being able to say what they think, you'll see it represents unprecedented opportunity.

It's ironic that these big corporates spend a fortune on market research and focus groups while all of the feedback they need is right under their noses, and what's more, it's free! Criticism is hard to take, even when constructive, however the fact people care enough to criticise or complain is a good thing; it would be far worse if nobody cared at all.

We should be encouraging and, in fact, facilitating feedback as often as we can - whether it's through social media, feedback forms on your website, surveying past clients, allowing reviews of your products to be posted on your website - every scrap of feedback is valuable information that most small businesses typically wouldn't have the budget for.

Of course we're focusing on the negatives here, however if your products and service are actually good then chances are that the feedback you attract will be good too! Positive, third-party feedback (testimonials, reviews, positive sentiment on social media channels) is worth its weight in gold, so stimulating that is a must!

Paying attention to the feedback you receive also gives you the opportunity to turn a negative into a positive. They say squeaky wheels make the most noise, and previously if someone was unhappy they'd go home, tell a whole bunch of their friends, and you'd be none the wiser. Now you have ways to tap in to those conversations and make things right. Often simply acknowledging and apologising for a grievance is enough to turn the situation around, and if you remedy it then you'll be surprised how often this can turn a dissenter into a die-hard advocate for your business.

So, make sure you're facilitating, encouraging and paying attention to feedback from your customers, after all if it weren't for them none of us would have anything to do!

Fail spectacularly

46

About 5 years ago I screwed up big on a project. I was a victim of inexperience, complacency and, perhaps, arrogance, and as a result I didn't deliver what was expected.

I had a number of choices - lie, pass the buck, or own up. I've already said in this book that I'm terrible at lying, I had nobody to pass the buck to, and I'm a pretty straight-cut bloke anyway so I fessed up and told the client I'd dropped the ball. This was a time sensitive project and this monumental screw-up was multiplied as it left the client in a bind with only 3 days to go before a big event they'd planned, for which they needed this website.

Obviously I had to rectify things, and so worked my backside off morning noon and night for those 3 days, rebuilding everything from scratch and cramming 2 months of work into 72 hours. Exhausted, and with dangerous levels of Red Bull and Pro Plus coursing around my body, I managed to turn it all around, delivered exactly what the client wanted, and the event went ahead successfully.

In my mind, I'd dodged a bullet and nearly killed myself to make it right. The strangest thing was, however, that in the eyes of this client I'd saved the day.

She was so appreciative of my honesty and grateful for my ability to resolve things in time that the fact I'd messed up in the first place seemed to be forgotten.

I went on to work with the client for a further year, and she still comes back to me when she needs more assistance, and she became a huge advocate of my work. I personally do not believe that this would have happened if it weren't for that massive road-bump I was able to navigate us both around.

Now don't get me wrong, I'm not advocating intentionally screwing things up as a marketing strategy! However we all make mistakes, the important thing is how we address them, and within that lays an opportunity to garner a much greater level of support and adoration from clients than would have been possible had everything gone to plan in the first place.

Naturally I've learned a lot from that experience and haven't made the same mistake since - however like all businesses there have been the occasional hiccups over the years. Any time something has gone wrong, however minor, I make it my first priority to "save the day" in spectacular fashion, and it's always turned out positive for everyone involved.

So next time you slip up, make sure that you own the problem and strive to resolve it with gusto!

Be the hero

47

In my previous tip I talked about turning mistakes into positive outcomes - however there are plenty more opportunities to be the hero to your clients that don't require you to have been the one who has messed up!

I've had a number of clients come to me for help when their website has been hacked. In most cases the remedial action is straightforward and so helping out isn't a huge job for me; however with the level of panic the typical website owner feels when their site has been hacked, the payoff for helping get someone out of that hole is huge.

Something else I come across often are cases where somebody has hired a web designer who has disappeared before completing the job. In these instances I've been able to either advise them on how to approach the situation, or have been able to pick the job up and finish it off successfully for them. Even though in those instances I get paid for my time, the fact that I've helped them out of a problematic situation garners gratitude far greater than that of an average project.

The web development industry is one rife with cowboys, and so the opportunities to be the hero are plentiful. Look to your industry for the sort of problems which occur all too often, and capitalise on your ability to help those who have been affected.

A great example of this was following the controversy over Endowment Policies just a few years ago, where people had either been misled or had misinterpreted the return on their investment, and many of them used their policy as security for mortgages - meaning when the payouts were less than expected these people faced the very real risk of losing their homes.

Savvy financial advisors were able to swoop in and guide people to a positive resolution. While they weren't necessarily able to recoup money which people were expecting, the fact that many were able to help those with problems to better navigate the situation won them a lot of favour and repeat business.

Keep your eyes open and your ears to the ground for opportunities to be the hero - nobody in their right mind gets annoyed with someone for rescuing them from a fire!

Smile and say hello

48

This is probably as simple a tip as you are going to read in this book, yet it is so under-utilised! Never underestimate the power of being polite, personable and pleasant!

There's no better way of doing that than simply smiling and saying hello to the people who work around you. Now of course I'm picturing a whole load of people reading this suddenly walking around with a deranged grin on their face, so perhaps don't go over the top with this, but if you work in say a shared office block or a business park, then just being friendly can create the tiniest of foundations upon which to strike up a conversation and a relationship later on down the road.

My friends Mark Bryant and Kelly-Anne Scott from the Media Partnership in Newcastle (www.mediapartnership.co.uk) decided to make an effort to try this within their office complex; and for an entire week made a concerted effort to smile, acknowledge and say hello to people from other businesses as they passed them by. After some initial confused looks they quickly found that those people would smile and say hello to them next time they passed them, and that conversations were starting in the queue at the cafe and the vending machines where usually everyone would be stood in silence.

These inevitably led to discussions about what they did, whereabouts in the complex they were based; and has gone on to lead to actual work coming from people they'd engaged with! Crazy when you think that all it took to get that process started was a smile.

So give it a shot, do what Mark and Kelly did, try making a conscious effort for a week and see where it gets you!

Spectacular gifts

49

I was in two minds about whether to include this one, given that the theme of this book is marketing on a budget, however I love this tip so much I thought it deserved it's place; and in terms of the potential return on something like this the costs involved could well be a drop in the ocean compared to what it results in.

I'm writing this only a week since Steve Jobs, founder and visionary behind Apple, sadly passed away. Poignant, then, that this tip is based on the incomparable appeal and desire he managed to cultivate for his products.

Tablet computers, and particularly the Apple iPad, are extremely desirable and somewhat "flashy" products and many businesses are starting to take advantage of that with a simple yet highly effective strategy. When sending proposals for high-value contracts; rather than take the typical route of spending an age preparing their proposal document and then spending a minute printing it out onto flimsy paper, some companies have taken the ingenious route of sending them out in PDF format on an iPad.

The rub, and the massive "wow" factor for the recipients, is that they get to keep the iPad!

It may seem like madness, but consider that you can pick up the basic iPad 2 for around £400, if the potential contract is worth several thousand then it becomes a small price to pay. Proposals submitted by your competitors will have to be pretty damn impressive to top sending it with a free iPad; and the potential poetry of your client emailing competitors to tell them their proposal has been rejected from the very iPad you sent them is too good to ignore!

Of course in the spirit of this book I'd be remiss if I didn't suggest that budget alternatives to the iPad should also be considered. Thanks to the phenomenal success of Apple's tablet, we now have a market ripe with alternatives; from entry-level alternatives starting from around £100, through to other high end competitors at the same price point.

It's less about the iPad – or an alternative – and more about being creative about creating that "wow" factor that sets you apart from the rest of the pack.

Call answering services

50

It shocked me to find out that 90% of people who are made to leave a voicemail message when trying to ring a company and give them business will never call back. Most of you reading this book will, like me, be a one man band. Yes you may use subcontractors and work with various partners but ultimately chances are you won't have a fully staffed office complete with receptionist to answer every call.

When I first heard that stat I started looking into what can be done about it, and came across a lot of online advice pointing me in the direction of hiring a virtual assistant, which I duly did. Problem was, however, that the VA was also a one man band, and since I wasn't paying enough to have her tied to a chair 24/7, calls still went missing.

The decision to outsource call answering for those times I was busy was vindicated, however, by a client who informed me that out of 6 companies he rang, mine was the only one where he managed to speak to a real person rather than a voicemail, even if that person wasn't me! That project ended up being worth £7000, the call cost me £1.25 to have answered and dealt with by my VA at the time.

However like I said, entrusting call answering to a one man band virtual assistant doesn't really solve the problem, and around the time I decided to cancel my contract I came across JAM (www.jam.co.uk), a Hertfordshire company offering call answering services. Not only do they have plenty of staff (all of whom sound infinitely better than I do on the phone!), but they work out cheaper than any other company - VA's included.

It's not so much about trying to portray yourself as bigger than you are by giving the impression that you have that big office with the receptionist, but just being realistic about the fact that most of the time you're not going to be able to answer the majority of calls yourself, and that this can lead to either losing potential business, or existing customers quickly growing tired of having a working relationship with your voicemail.

A good call answering service will be able to answer the phone according to instructions which you set, as well as offer call patching, SMS/email notifications, and details on how to deal with specific callers or types of calls (I.e. putting certain clients straight through, and fobbing off people calling to sell you something).

Without a doubt the best practical decision I ever made for my business from early on was to utilise a third party to answer calls when I wasn't available, and it turned out to be a fantastic marketing decision too; one which I always recommend people consider.

Car boot customers

51

I managed to go for 24 years of my life never having attended a car boot sale, until one freezing cold morning in March 2007 I loaded my car up with junk and headed out at 6am. Truthfully, I loved it! I sold most of my stuff - mainly DVD's and computer games - before lunchtime, and walked away with £200 to go towards buying more DVD's and computer games which I'd inevitably sell a few years later, at another car boot sale!

Setting aside the fact that I'd probably paid more than £2000 for all the stuff that had been sold, I was happy - instant gratification, cash in my hand, and everything sold. Result.

So I went back the next weekend, and the next, and the next - for two months I raided my cupboards for stuff I could sell - not because I needed to, just because I enjoyed the satisfaction and experience, and because I had a lot of tat to get rid of!

The more I did it, the poorer the selection of stuff I had was, yet it was still selling - however I noticed a pattern forming... When I was flogging off my DVD box sets for £3 a pop, it didn't strike me as odd when people tried to do deals, or to haggle down to £2.50; however weeks later when I was selling junk, I was getting people trying to haggle me down from 40p to 30p; and not jokingly or in a tongue-in-cheek way, they were deadly serious about making that 10p saving!

This made me think back to my first car boot experience and how proud I was of myself for being such a great salesman that I cleared all of my "stock" within just a few hours. Of course I did, because I was practically giving them away! However even though I was selling at such a stupidly low price, people wanted it to be lower still, and we're willing to spend a good 15-20 minutes arguing for their right to have it cheaper before shuffling off with barely a thank you after I'd eventually caved.

While recovering from my shameful Sunday morning addiction, I thought a lot about the sort of buyer mentality I'd witnessed, and considered it in the context of people I'd encountered in my business. The ones who would express shock and outrage at the fact I wouldn't build them a website for £100, and would actually try to make me feel bad about it! Ones who would haggle over the tiniest points just to save a minimal amount off their bill, and those who went to a competitor even though they knew their work was inferior to mine, simply because they were a couple of hundred pound cheaper.

I came to label those types of people as car boot customers.

It's because of car boot customers that Groupon, once heralded as the future of online buying, is now facing an enormous backlash from retailers and companies who have been encouraged to compromise their business sensibilities for the promise of an influx of hitherto unreachable customers. These companies quickly found that the scavenging, car boot nature of most of these customers meant that many of them were far more demanding than full paying customers, and very rarely turned into repeat business.

Don't let car boot customers force you into devaluing yourself and your business for the sake of a quick win.

Use a CRM system

52

I have a terrible memory; it's absolutely shocking - I can remember events from years ago with intricate detail but when it comes to remembering a conversation from a day or so ago I completely... hang on, what I was talking about?

It's not as drastic as I make out, but I have been caught with my pants down a few times in the past where a potential customer has asked me to call them and it's completely slipped out of my mind, only to return 3 days later, or when they've emailed me to tell me they've gone with another supplier.

Fortunately though, I've found a solution to my problem, one which every business should consider using, and that's a CRM system.

For those who don't know, CRM stands for Customer Relationship Management, and does exactly what it says on the tin, facilitates the management of your customer relationships. I'd always assumed that such systems were for high-end corporates, however they do come in handy even for one man bands, and while some systems are extremely complex, there is also some fantastic slimmed down software on the market more suited to smaller businesses.

A typical CRM system will have the following features:

- Ability to add and manage contact details for clients
- The facility to add dated notes (and files) to client records
- the ability to create and schedule "tasks" for yourself, in relation to a client, and to prompt you when those tasks are due (such as "call Joe Bloggs")

There are, naturally, a range of other useful features found in many of the small business CRM solutions - project management tools, sales pipeline tracking etc - however at a basic level, and for the purposes of keeping your finger on the pulse of customer activity, the features outlined above are the main ones you need.

I always have my CRM open on my computer, and have access to it through my mobile phone and iPad too, and after every conversation or email exchange with a customer I add a quick note about what we discussed to their record in my CRM. If I've agreed to call them or do something for them, such as email them a file etc., I'll also set myself a task to remind me and prompt me to follow up.

I also make sure that I add any new contacts to my CRM, for example when I'm out networking new people I meet who pass me their business card go into my CRM with a note about where I met them, what they do etc. Some use this for pure sales purposes - I do it more to remind myself and give me quick access to someone's contact information. My CRM contacts automatically transfer to my phone, so if someone I've just recently met tries to call me, their name pops up, helping my avoid the initial "who the hell is this?" process!

I've used a multitude of different small-business CRM systems over the years, and my personal preferences are Highrise (www.highrisehq.com) and Capsule (www.capsulecrm.com) - both web-based, subscription software.

Highrise is from 37Signals, developers of Basecamp, and well recognised as one of the leading small business software companies around. As such, their CRM is a fantastic system: easy to use, rich in features, and integrates well with a range of other software. However the sticking point is their pricing, which can be a little too much if you're not using it a lot or don't have a huge amount of customers or activity to log.

The alternative, and my current weapon of choice, is Capsule which - while not looking as good and not being quite as slick as Highrise - has an impressive feature set, including some that Highrise doesn't have such as sales pipeline logs etc. My favourite thing with Capsule, however, is how well it integrates into Google Apps (apps.google.com), mainly the email side of things, which makes the whole contact management process so much easier.

Both have a free trial so you can check them out for yourself, but whichever one you choose the important thing is that you have something, anything, in place to help you manage your customer relationships, and most important of all, that you actually use it!

Ask for testimonials

53

I've never really understood why so many business owners have an issue with the idea of actively requesting testimonials. Being able to prove that you're not the only person who thinks you're fantastic carries a lot of weight, so why wouldn't you ask your past clients for feedback?

The act of actually requesting testimonials can be daunting for some people. If you are one of those who are put off by the idea consider sending an email rather than asking over the phone or in person, that way if somebody doesn't want to leave you a testimonial then it's a fairly non-pressured approach which they can choose to follow up on if they want to.

For the shy ones among us – look for natural opportunities to gather a testimonial. For example if a customer openly says something positive about you or your business, ask them whether they'd have time to put that in writing; or if they've made these positive comments in an email, ask them whether they'd mind you quoting it verbatim, or whether they'd mind expanding on it for you to use on your website.

You may want to consider making testimonial gathering part of your standard processes, whether that is a letter you send to clients, a follow up call, or a form on your website. Contacting past clients for testimonials is also a great way to stoke the fires of a relationship which has gone off the boil, and could lead to upselling opportunities.

As important as testimonials are, whatever you do please don't make the ill-judged decision some others do, and make up fake testimonials. Not only is it dishonest, but it'll be obvious to readers and won't do anything other than make you look stupid.

Of course once you have testimonials, make sure you show them off! Choose some of the best to use in your promotional materials, put them on your website, and if you've gathered testimonials on sites such as LinkedIn or 4Networking, consider including a link to them in your email signatures.

If you're in a business which produces and sends proposals and quotations, it only takes a few more minutes to hand pick some appropriate testimonials to go along with it. If you network a lot, consider having a testimonials book which you can display; and do the same if you run a hotel, restaurant etc.

Many will tell you that word of mouth is one of the most effective means of marketing, and being able to "capture" that in the form of written testimonials is a no-brainer!

Every contact counts

54

They say it takes an average of 7 "touches" in order to make a sale. Of course you'll have those people who buy immediately, and there'll be those who you "work on" for months, but on average it works out as around 7 connections.

At one point this was challenging; meetings, phone calls and letters were pretty much the only means of contacting a customer, and so making those connections could be a bit of a slog. These days, however, it's easier than ever thanks to technology.

Now don't get me wrong, tweeting someone 7 times isn't likely to land a sale, you still need to engage your brain at some point, but the tools at your disposal are more varied than ever. By interspersing social media and email marketing into the more traditional means of engaging a customer the whole process becomes more manageable.

It doesn't even need to be a direct engagement either - if you meet someone at a networking event and take their card, with permission to add them to your email list, then follow this up with a short email saying how great it was to meet them; then connect with them on twitter - not only are you directly contacting them, but they'll also be seeing your email marketing campaigns, as well as seeing your name pop up on twitter, Facebook and the like - even if you're not directly addressing them.

This repetition breeds recognition, so next time you see them, or if you call them the following week, foundations have been built and you've been in "their world" on and off without actually being there. The tools to keep a conversation going are more varied than ever, so make sure you're using them to keep your engagements flowing.

Your Website

These next 3 sections all deal with the online world. I did initially wonder whether this was a bit too much "web stuff" for one book; however the biggest tool in the small business marketing arsenal is the massive potential represented by marketing your business online.

This is particularly true with the notion of "Bootstrap" – low cost and no cost marketing techniques. The Internet is ripe with potential for this very approach to marketing, and if you're looking to promote your business effectively on a budget then you'll need to harness the power of online marketing.

While online marketing and social media are massive components of small business marketing, your website needs to be at the heart of these activities, and it's often one of the main things most small businesses get wrong.

Let's get this out of the way first – my main business is one which specialises in website design and online strategy; so while it makes sense that this would be an area in which I have the most insight to share, doing so isn't a deliberate ploy, nor does it mean I'm giving undue emphasis to my "pet interests" over other marketing avenues. Online marketing truly is the most potent means of marketing a small business, and hopefully this becomes evident throughout the following sections.

But let's get back to your website. We've long since moved past the point where business owners need to be convinced of the necessity of having a website – however when first starting up not only is your website one of a long list of things demanding your attention, but often people simply do not have the budget to hire a professional.

Even when money isn't an issue, choosing the right approach and indeed the right company is a minefield; and in the rare instance where you get everything right, simply having a good website isn't enough if it's not utilised correctly and has been created devoid of any strategy.

This section aims to help you navigate through all of this – to get the best from anyone you hire to build your website, or indeed to build it yourself; and ensure that once you actually have a website in place, you make good use of it.

Choose your domain name wisely
by Dickie Armour

55

One of the first things any online business must make sure is that they are using a proper domain name. Don't use a URL that comes with your free hosting eg: mywebsite.freehost.co.uk It looks really unprofessional. Buy a domain name which reflects your business brand and company name, eg www.bmc-media.co.uk A domain name costs no more than £9 a year and gives your business a much more professional brand and image.

I use my personal name for my main website - www.dickiearmour.me.uk I use the .me.uk domain name extension because I was standing in the Nominet non-executive director elections a few years ago and as it's a website about me, I chose to use the .me.uk as that's what it was created for.

So if you are your business it's fine to use your name. I can't remember who told me this but it is so true - you are the Richard Branson of your business. So using your name as your website is great. Authors and actors and celebrities are the main types of people who use their own names in their website address but a lot more people are now doing the same for their businesses.

One other thing to consider if you're launching a new online business is don't forget to check with companies house to see if the company name is still available too. At the outset, you may not be planning on a limited company; you might be happy trading as a sole trader or a partnership. But you should still check because one day you might decide to change to a limited company and it would be a shame if the limited company name was not available.

At first glance you might not be able to register the exact domain name you want but there are many different alternatives. If you wanted to register massivemarketingmagic.co.uk and massivemarketingmagic.com but one or other were taken, you could use a hyphen (-) in between the words. Massive-marketing-magic.co.uk and massive-marketing-magic.com instead. Sometimes it's easier to read and understand a domain name if a hyphen has been used.

Also look out for some of those simple to make mistakes by using a domain which could cause offence. It's easy not to realise what your domain name looks like when joined together.

Check out these examples:

Pen Island
Experts Exchange
Who Represents

They all look quite innocent don't they? But look what happens when you see them as a website address!!

www.penisland.net
www.expertsexchange.com
www.whorepresents.com

So make sure you check how your chosen domain looks as a website address!

Dickie Armour is an author, speaker, entrepreneur and non-executive director at Nominet.
www.dickiearmour.me.uk

Get the best from your web designer

56

While the Bootstrap mentality is mainly based around marketing your business on a shoestring, there will be areas where bringing in a pro is the best move for your business. If the development of your website is one of those areas, then you need to know that hiring someone to design and/ or build your website can be a bit of a minefield; and even with the best of website development companies at the helm, projects can sometimes go awry.

With that in mind, this "tip" actually consists of 5 "mini-tips" aimed at helping you as a client get the best from your website development company:

Put things into perspective

Some of the biggest causes of disappointment when a business has their website built stem from expectations being too high about what that site will do for them. Whether this is down to the client misunderstanding where their site will fit into their marketing strategy, or whether it is the website developers over-promising the "end-results", it is important to put your website into perspective and truly understand the realistic impact it will have.

Simply having a website built will not revolutionise your business – it is merely a tool (albeit a potentially powerful one) in your marketing arsenal, and needs to be used correctly to be effective.

Work with your developer on a sitemap and plan

Your website developer will typically plot out a "sitemap", which will outline the various sections, features and processes on your site. This is usually done right at the start of the project, so it pays to discuss this together and ensure that both parties fully understand how the site will shape up and what its capabilities are so nothing is forgotten and there are no nasty surprises when the site is finished.

Provide plenty of information and content

If your project relies on you providing the content; getting this to your website developer as early as possible will have a positive effect on development; as otherwise they will be working with dummy/filler content, as well as possibly structuring certain parts of your site on assumptions about how you want it to work. Ensuring you provide any written content, imagery and outlines will help things to go much smoother.

Ask your developer to create a live testing environment

Some website developers test and update the "in-development" version of your site in a live online location; whereas others develop it "locally" (i.e. on their own in-house systems). If at all possible, ask your developers to set up a live online version of the site during development which you can access. This enables you to view and use the site as it is being built, allowing you to flag any issues early rather than having to wait until the end of the project to test everything – at which point people typically feel pressured into "signing off" the project and getting it live.

Communicate

Ultimately, if you want to get the best from your website developer, you need to talk to them. Yes, I know a lot of us are odd, smelly, anti-social beings who sometimes find it hard to string together a sentence without it involving some form of code; but keep in touch with your developer throughout the project. Agree "milestones" – points during the project when you'll sit down together and discuss progress. Establish the best way to communicate with each other in terms of what works best for each of you – whether that be daily emails or a once a week phone call. Communication is the absolute key to ensuring that the website developed is the website you want.

Hopefully this gives you a bit of food for thought if you're considering having your website developed or revamped; or maybe you've had a bit of a rough experience with your web developer and you can now see where things may have fallen down. Whatever the case, I hope this helps.

Keep your site updated

57

Just a quick tip when it comes to your website; if you have a blog or news section (which you should do as it is a great way to publish fresh content and boost SEO), and find yourself unable to keep it up to date regularly; then consider asking your website developer to remove the date on which the news/blog entry was posted.

The reason I suggest this is because if you haven't updated your blog in a while, the only measure a visitor has of how recent the activity in your business has been is the dates of your blog updates; and if your last update was in 2009, what are they going to think?

In all likelihood, they'll assume you've gone out of business, because it doesn't look like you've "been around" for 3 years!

I've built sites with news sections where the "latest news" is still "Welcome to our website"...

Don't cheapen your website

58

Picture the scene... You've put a lot of time and effort into convincing someone to come and meet you to listen to what you have to offer them, they've taken time out of their day to come to your office, and as they walk in, admiring the decor, you motion them towards a nice comfy chair opposite a plush leather sofa. You walk over to the sofa, pause for a second, and then begin frantically digging down the back of it, rummaging around. They sit there, bemused at first, and growing increasingly irritated by the second. Finally you stop rummaging and pull out a grubby 10 pence piece, holding it aloft triumphantly before shoving it into your back pocket and sitting down with a proud smile on your face.

How do you think the rest of that meeting will play out?

As ludicrous as it sounds, there are loads of business owners who are effectively doing the above when it comes to their website. They go to the effort and expensive of having a fancy site built and the painstaking process of driving traffic to it, only for it to be littered with third party adverts. That's tantamount to rummaging around for spare change when you've got a real sales opportunity sitting right in front of you.

Having third party adverts on your business site is probably the biggest faux pas I've ever come across in terms of online marketing. It tells me that you're not good enough at what you do to make enough money and that you're so lacking in pride in your business and your brand that you're willing to cheapen yourself for the sake of a few extra pounds per month.

Don't get me wrong, I'm not talking about people who run standalone blogs, or companies with sponsorships and endorsements; I mean the brochure site with a whole bunch of ugly Google ads shoved into every free space there is, or worse, banner ads! There's no conceivable reason why anyone should ever consider this a sensible thing to do with their website, yet you wouldn't believe how many people have asked me to implement this for them on their site (I've flat out refused, every time).

To a lesser extent this also applies to link exchanges too - where you've agreed to put a link to someone else's website on yours in exchange for them doing the same. Often people who do this do it with a number of other sites, so you end up with a long list of completely irrelevant links which make zero sense to your visitors and distract them from your core message.

The biggest example of this is something called "Freeindex", an online directory to which entry is secured by sticking their hideous button on your site. This just looks cheap and tacky, and guess what? It makes your business look cheap and tacky too.

Another of the most common places you find this is on sites where people have used free templates, often for Wordpress. As free template makers obviously don't make money from the distribution of their templates they recoup it in other ways, typically by selling a number of sponsored link areas on the bottom of this design. These are typically available for anyone to buy and tend to be advertised in places populated by web marketers clawing for ways to get their own junk websites advertised; and so your fancy accountancy practice which uses one of these templates ends up having their website "sponsored" by a range of online gambling and sex pill websites!

When you consider that a high quality and link-free Wordpress template can be bought for around £20-30 then having ads really doesn't send a great message.

So whatever you do, please do not undo any of the hard work you or your web designer has done by cheapening your website and your business with daft stuff like this!

Turn your website into a resource

59

Chances are you won't want to hear this, but your fancy new "brochure" website? The one you either paid a fortune for or spent hours painstakingly crafting yourself? Nobody cares about it...

This is a harsh reality that very few web people will tell you at the outset (because they don't want to devalue their work). Having a website these days is no longer a big deal, it no longer puts you ahead of the competition, it simply brings you in line with them. If, like many others, your site simply covers the "who", "where", "what" and "why" of your business, then ask yourself, why should anybody other than you give a monkeys?

So, you've invested in this spanking new website that nobody cares about, what can you do about it? The answer is obvious - give them something they will care about!

By turning your website into a resource which provides something people want - be it information, freebies or tools they can use - you provide an incentive for people to visit regardless of whether they know about your business or have an interest in what it is you do and sell.

But do you want to attract people who have no interest in buying from you? Of course you do! Because while they may not want or need to buy from you today, they may need to in 12 months time; and if they've been a regular reader of, for example, your blog about wood-burning stoves, and then later find they need to buy one, you've already built that association and trust in their mind so you will be their first port of call.

Having a blog which you use to share advice and information about a particular field is the simplest way of turning your website into a resource; particularly if you don't hold back, and actually "reveal" some of the information which you may have a natural urge to charge for. Research has shown that with the vast majority of people even when you give them all the details on how to do something themselves, they still won't bother - however the willing sharing of that information will go a long way to build trust.

Alternatively you could offer free downloads; eBooks, white papers, research etc; if you are a recruitment company you could offer interview tips and CV templates; financial planners could offer free calculation spreadsheets and budget templates; car valeting companies could offer videos showing how to detail clean your own car, and so on.

Transforming your website from a run-of-the-mill promotional tool to a genuinely useful resource is powerful stuff, and even if the majority of people using that resource will never have a need to purchase from or otherwise do business with you, they will be out there sharing your content and advocating you, your business and your website.

As I said previous having a website no longer puts you ahead of your competitors. Now, in order to achieve that, you don't need a website, you need a web resource.

Call to action

60

This is perhaps the biggest mistake I see people make when it comes to marketing and sales. For all their fancy marketing materials and suave sales patter, they forget one crucial thing - the "close", the "call to action".

When it comes to face to face sales this usually materialises in them simply avoiding (or forgetting) to do a little thing called asking for the sale! This is perhaps somewhat understandable - not everyone enjoys or is good at sales and there is an unwarranted fear about actually asking someone outright whether they are going to buy your product. That's a topic to be explored in someone else's book, but ultimately the advice is to just bloody do it!

Where it is more frustrating is when people don't have a call to action on their sales literature and, particularly, their website.

First and foremost you need to actually determine what it is you want people to do. Do you want them to buy something? Book something? Download something? Provide feedback? Share something? Or maybe just pick up the phone? Identify what it is you want people to do as the ultimate end result from their use of your website, and build your call to action around that.

It is entirely possible that you may want them to do one of several things - either place an order, call you, or share your website; in which case you need to prioritise and ensure that this is reflected on your site; but don't overdo it, too many calls to action for different things will pull your visitors from pillar to post, and they are more likely to just bugger off to a competitors site rather than persevere and try to figure out what you want them to do.

When it comes to business websites, most of them are straightforward brochure sites which don't sell a product, and where the only real course of action a potential customer could be guided to take is to pick up the phone and make an enquiry. However, even with something so simple I'm continuously amazed how many websites don't have a phone number available, or any other means of contact for that matter! This is such a basic mistake to remedy so if you don't have your phone number on your website, put this book down and go and sort it out now!

Ultimately it all comes back to purpose. What is the purpose of your website, how can visitors fulfil that purpose, and what do you need to do to facilitate that. Without a clear purpose you can't establish clear calls to action, and without those your website is basically just a pretty little appendage that will never do anything for your business.

Off the shelf websites

61

I'm going to tell you something that could be seen as a little bit crazy considering I run a web design company; something so shocking that it could very well get me kicked out of the Secret Society of Web Designers...

Most small businesses should not be paying more than £1000 for a website.

Hell, most shouldn't even be paying more than £500-£600!

Now before my office is petrol-bombed by a thousand angry geeks, let me qualify this. Something a lot of web designers have no concept of is the fact that when starting out a business, sorting out a website is just one of a long list of things you need to do. Yes, it is important, and yes you absolutely must have a website, but when you consider the expenses which quickly stack up versus the slow-moving nature of winning your first clients and actually getting money in the bank, it's crazy to spend thousands of pounds on a new website.

Don't get me wrong, the websites that cost thousands typically do so for a reason. Web design is a much more complex field than many realise - part art-form, part science. Good web design encompasses many different variables such as quality design, technical considerations, usability, sales psychology, accessibility, future-proofing and so on. Good quality web design takes time, and time costs money, money that most small businesses don't have.

The argument could be made that since your website is an investment, you should invest a lot of money with a view to make that back tenfold; however from a standing start, unless your website performs some sort of functional or transactional task it is not going to be much more than a fancy digital brochure, and as such isn't going to help open the floodgates to instant profits. So unless your website enables people to book something, order something or buy something, i.e. something which will directly make you money, then throwing money you don't have at it sounds crazy, and even if you do have that money, chances are it could be spent to better effect elsewhere.

However, you do still need a website, and a good quality one at that... It's a bit of a pickle...

Thankfully there is a solution, one which die-hard web geeks will hate, but one which makes business sense. Buy your website "off the shelf".

A few years ago the notion of using a pre made template was a ridiculous one; the vast majority of templates available were low quality and typically quite high cost. Editing them or using them in any real way required knowledge of HTML, which contradicted the point of using them in the first place. The design was often cheesy and clichéd, the code was often messy.

Recently, however, the entire field has changed thanks to a few core sites leading the way for high quality, low cost templates.

It's not all about the design however; the "engine" of the site is of equal importance if you actually want to be able to keep your website up to date with a content management system.

The most popular open source (read: free) content management system platform is Wordpress. Wordpress started life as a blogging platform but has evolved so much that millions of websites use it to control all elements of the site content. There's little you can do with a bespoke, custom coded solution that you can't do with Wordpress.

Wordpress also benefits from there being thousands of templates available for it, many designed by some of the world's best web designers who make their money through selling in volume, or selling memberships to websites offering their templates. My personal preferences/recommendations for places to purchase a quality Wordpress template would be ThemeForest (who also sell thousands of plain HTML templates as well as templates for other off the shelf systems), WooThemes (who sell memberships to access all of their templates, as well as the ability to make individual purchases) and ElegantThemes (who sell a cheap yearly membership to access all of their themes).

Most of these themes come with comprehensive instructions - however I'd be lying if I said that setting up Wordpress and installing a theme was a cakewalk for someone who is a self-confessed Luddite; so there may still be the need to involve someone who knows what they're doing.

The big difference is, if you hire a web designer/developer to install and set up Wordpress with a pre made template, you're paying them for the time it takes to assemble pre-prepared "ingredients", rather than them having to actually create and build something from scratch - so the costs should be minimal. I tend to compare this to a chef cooking a meal. You don't go into a restaurant expecting your steak to be cut from a cow which has been freshly killed in the kitchen! Instead you pay your money for someone to put together high quality ingredients (Wordpress, your chosen template) to create a meal (your website).

It is important that you recognise the downsides, however. Firstly a website crafted this way will never be 100% suited to your needs, you won't be able to customise it very much or have some of the bespoke functionality you may want. You'll have to accept the fact that there may be a few dozen, maybe a few hundred other sites out there using the same template too.

You should also view this as a temporary solution - at some point in your business you should look at bringing in a professional to create something more fitting to your business and your objectives - however by that point having had a website that doesn't look like your brothers cousins babysitters dog built it should give you a stronger basis upon which to work towards something great.

In the meantime, however, if it's a question of not having a website, designing one yourself, or following this advice and using something like Wordpress with a high quality template, I'm sure even those pitchfork carrying, die-hard web geeks currently programming my address into their sat nav would find it hard to disagree that the latter is the best option.

Online Marketing

A good friend and one of the smartest business men I know – Paul Norman (Orangetree Development) – once talked to me of the "global village". He observed that hundreds of years ago we all lived in little villages; everyone knew who their local butcher or baker were, and would walk from one end of the village to the other in order to buy what they needed.

That village still exists, only now – thanks to the Internet – it's on a global scale. Communities flourish and thrive online, and the connectivity of the World Wide Web means that it's still a simple "stroll" to get to the person selling what we need, even when they're in a different country.

Making effective use of online marketing in order to set out your stall in that "village" is one of the best ways a small business can market and establish themselves online. The ability to reach thousands upon thousands of people at the click of a mouse, and draw in people who you would otherwise never have had the opportunity to reach, is a priceless commodity.

It's testament to the potency of online marketing that there are a million and one (probably more!) blogs, eBooks, training courses and the like out there, all giving a different view on how to best market your business online. And of course in the name of peeing in the ocean, I'm doing the very same thing here! However, unlike much of the advice that's around, this is based on experience, research, and isn't tainted by attempts to swindle you out of money for an even more expensive and "revolutionary" eBook, course or blog!

It's entirely feasible to build an entire business using online marketing without ever spending a penny – and indeed there are hundreds of thousands of people out there who have done just that. The tools and opportunities are out there, accessible to all – it's down to you to make use of them!

Easy Email Marketing

62

I bet when you picked up this book you had no idea I'd be changing your fortunes forever... Well it just so happens that I've recently had an email from a Nigerian prince who's having difficulty transferring a large sum of cash...

Okay, so you're not going to fall for that one (again?), but plenty have, and that's just one of the reasons why email marketing has received such bad publicity over recent years.

There is, however, a wealth of potential in email marketing if, and only if, it is done correctly. First things first - firing out a few lines from Microsoft Outlook is not the right way to do things. Years of being bombarded with spam has led to increased paranoia, so if you want to get through to your recipient you'll get much further with well designed email templates.

I feel somewhat cheap recommending a "way around" professional email marketing services, since they're already very cost effective - however if you're working with zero budget then take a look at Mailchimp (www. mailchimp.com) - they offer a selection of free, quality templates, and for mailing lists of under a certain amount they will process your campaigns at no cost.

The downside to this is that they will include their link at the bottom of your emails; however it is fairly discreet and doesn't necessarily cheapen your message too much; and it doesn't cost a great deal to upgrade and remove their branding by taking on their pay monthly or pay as you go accounts.

Pay per click, without paying

63

For anyone considering paying for advertising online, Google Adwords is an absolute must. I'm a big fan of Google's pay-per-click advertising program, not only because of Google's massive user base, but also because few other forms of advertising offer the ability to only pay if someone takes the action you want them to - in this case visiting your website.

The fact that you can control every aspect of your spending, manage and limit your budgets, and analyse and adjust your marketing activity in real time makes this a great option for smaller businesses or companies with a limited budget.

If you're considering using Google Adwords, however, here's a quick tip. There's an extremely popular magazine for people in the web development community called .Net - which typically includes a Google Adwords voucher within almost every issue. These vouchers vary in value, but are usually for £50 if redeemed before a certain date, and £30 thereafter.

When you consider that the magazine itself costs just over £5, it is well worth the trip to WH Smith's to pick up a copy and grab yourself £50 worth of Adwords credit!

While this is a promotion which .Net have been running for years there is, of course, the chance that this may cease at some point in the future. Don't fear, as there are plenty of other places which offer free Adwords vouchers. Everyone from SEO companies to business bank accounts, to web hosting providers tend to throw in Adwords vouchers as an incentive – though obviously these are dependent on you signing up for their services. Scouring online business forums, however, will often turn up people offering them either completely free, or for a small charge – you just need to do a bit of digging.

For now though, a trip to the newsagents is all you need!

Affiliate schemes

64

This isn't something which will be doable for everyone, but if you sell a product or a packaged service online, then one of the most effective ways of channelling new business is to run an affiliate scheme.

What this means is that if someone clicks on one of your partners links, visits your site and buys your product; then that partner will get either a fixed amount or a percentage of that sale.

It's a widely used strategy employed successfully by some of the largest online businesses (Amazon have one of the most established and successful affiliate schemes), and there is a wide selection of software available which enables you to set up and run your own scheme (or alternatively you can look to offer it through companies who facilitate affiliate offers, such as Clickbank).

What this does is give you a way to create advocates for your product or service who don't necessarily have to have tried it themselves. There will, of course, be a concern about whether that's a good thing, but essentially it's down to the affiliates themselves to determine whether they're happy to make a baseless recommendation. If you want to control this area a bit more you can have a closed affiliate scheme where people apply to take part, and adhere to certain guidelines.

Affiliate schemes are tried, tested and extremely effective - so if you have a product or service which lends itself to such a scheme, and is possible to sell online in an automated manner, then you really shouldn't be missing out on using affiliates yourself,

SEO made simple
by Gareth Mailer

65

"Search Engine Optimisation is about increasing the visibility of your website in search" – the definition is simple, and so too is the process (and particularly so if you're a small business owner).

When it comes to making SEO work, webmasters and business owners find it all too easy to end up lost in a myriad of jargon: "insert target keywords here", "build links there", "make sure your keyword density equals x" and so on. Forget it. All of it.

SEO can be boiled down into a collection of four factors:

Keyword Research: Treat search like a business model – target sales, not search volume. Some keywords are incredibly competitive, some aren't competitive at all. The trick? Target less competitive targeted keywords which actually drive search volume (and ultimately sales).

Accessibility: Make sure your website is accessible – search engines utilise web crawlers, which are essentially computer programs, to crawl the web. These crawlers "click" on the links on your website, and index your content. The long and the short of it? Make sure your pages fall no more than five clicks away from your homepage (your most authoritative and important page).

Content Development: Create unique, quality content for the purpose of informing your users and driving sales through your web presence (note the omission of "create content for search engines"). Create unique content for each of your main target terms (group relevant target terms together on one page e.g. "SEO Manchester",

"SEO Cheshire" etc).

Link Building: Link Building works out to be roughly 70% of all the activity you will be performing on your SEO Campaign – it's THAT important. Link building is so important that you could simply create a blank page of content (with no text or anything on it), and get it to rank in search simply by building links to it.

So, there you have it, the "process" behind Search Engine Optimisation summed up in just a few hundred words.

Gareth Mailer is a seasoned SEO specialist, delivering strategy and training through Clickwork Media
www.clickworkmedia.co.uk

Landing pages

66

A key mistake which many business owners make when they're setting up a website for their business is to focus all of their attentions on the homepage, or to assume that this is where they want their traffic to go.

This becomes a costly mistake when people fork out money for search engine optimisation or pay per click services with the intention of driving traffic to their homepage.

Unless you operate a one-page website, or have a company which only offers a single specific product or service, then in most cases your homepage is the absolute last place you want me to "land" on when I search for what you offer.

How often to you nip to the supermarket only needing to pick one thing up, and then have to hunt around for the right aisle? How much easier and more satisfying would it be if, when you walked through the door, the exact item you wanted was nicely laid out right in front of you?

If I do a search for draught excluders, see your site at the top of the search results and eagerly click through, it is a major pain if I land on the homepage and then have to spend time digging around your site to find the right page. If, however, that search result linked directly to the page on your site which dealt with draught excluders then I'd be a happy bunny, and more likely to buy from you.

For every service and product that you and your company offer there should be a comprehensive, well designed and well constructed landing page that tells me everything I might need to know about that specific thing and leads me to take whatever action you're trying to invoke -

whether that's making a purchase or simply picking up the phone. However so many people treat their actual product and service description pages as an afterthought.

Now of course your homepage does serve a purpose and should be well thought out - but that is there for the "window shoppers", the people who kind of just stumble onto your website, or go there with a purpose but don't know where to start or what they're looking for.

Think of it this way, if I'm looking to buy draught excluders (hey, it's cold up north!) and you have just one opportunity, one single page on your website, to get my business; what page should that be? What information should it contain? How should it look?

Ask yourself the same question – if you were looking for a particular service or product, what information would you like to see, or indeed expect to see on a website which purported to meet your needs? Now ask the same question with your customer in mind – if they're looking for what you're selling, what will they be expecting?

That's your landing page.

Have a content strategy

67

When it comes to marketing your business online, content truly is king. It is through content that you get your message across to your customers; content is a major factor in determining how well you rank in the search engines; and content is currency when it comes to having something to talk about and share through social media.

With such importance placed on content, however, it's easy to get lost in the middle of it all and end up adopting a scattergun approach. This can work in the short term but is akin to a "sugar high" and isn't great as a long term solution. What you need is a robust content strategy.

While this term implies something overly complex and corporate, it can be fairly simple. It's merely a case of planning out what you're going to say, and where and when you're going to say it.

Assuming you have a blog, Twitter account, Facebook account and have resolved to set up a YouTube channel and start publishing videos then you already have the tools at your disposal for a pretty solid content strategy. All you need to do now is sit down and decide how often you're going to update these channels, and what it is you're going to publish.

Personally I just use a simple spreadsheet, and set myself the task of publishing two blog posts and one video per week. So for every week I have a list with "blog, blog, video", and every three months or so I go through and put a title for a blog post or a video along with any short notes I may need to jog my memory.

It's much easier to come up with titles or half-conceived ideas in advance than it is to sit down and write an article from scratch; and so this approach gets rid of a large part of the worry about what I can actually write or talk about. If you're struggling to even think of titles, then the best way to get inspiration is to look at what others are discussing. Search for blogs in your field and "subscribe" to their RSS feeds using something like reader.google. com - this sends all the latest stories from blogs you've found into an inbox, and simply reviewing these every couple of days will give you food for thought, and insight into what people in the industry are discussing.

And so with a single spreadsheet I have a specific 3 month content strategy, consisting of 3 updates a week - each of which I then share on Twitter and post to Facebook. That's actually quite a lot of activity when you think about it, particularly compared to what a lot of others are doing.

In truth, my content strategy is a little more complex than that - however it's how mine started and is a good starting point for you too. Mine now consists of splitting blog posts into "standard" and "feature", which determines length and content styles. It also takes into account publishing blog articles on sites other than my own, as well as including the creation of eBooks, running email marketing campaigns, and a broader use of social media.

If you're in a larger business, or one with more than one member of staff, then your content strategy should also include details of who is going to create that content too.

Most businesses in general recognise the importance of content, however don't have the all important content strategy - so do yourself a favour and start on a basic one today before everyone else catches up!

Blog commenting

68

A common activity in the world of online marketing is strategically posting comments on the blogs of other people in your industry.

Use the search engines to find any blogs with comments enabled which rank highly for your targeted keywords, or even keywords you have opted not to directly target because they're too competitive.

Make sure you read the article (or enough of it to be able to post something constructive), and bear in mind that most comments on blogs need to be approved by the author before they're displayed, so it needs to add some value - a short paragraph commenting on the article content is enough.

The point of this is that the majority of blogging platforms enable you to link the name with which you post to you own website - so your comment will have a link going directly back to your site.

The benefits of this are numerous - firstly you'll get a bit of a rub on the SEO side of things for having your link on a well-ranked page; that "rub" is enhanced by the fact that the page on which you link appears has content relevant to that of your own site; and finally other people who are reading the article may very well click through and visit your site.

Be my guest

69

Publishing content is at the heart of any good online marketing strategy, so maintaining your own blog with quality articles is a must. However when doing so, remember that you are broadcasting to your own audience. That's not necessarily a bad thing, but a good strategy would be to spread yourself out a little and tap into the audiences of others too.

Participating as a guest blogger on somebody else's website has a multitude of benefits. Not only is it putting your views in front of new people, but it's also a fantastic way to build up your own personal profile as an industry expert. If somebody searches for you by name and sees a whole bunch of results showing blogs on your own site, then that's fine; but how much more impressive would it be if they saw your name associated with blogs all over the Internet?

The best place to start is to search for prominent bloggers in your industry, and approach them to see whether they accept guest contributors. If you actually check their site in advance you'll be able to ascertain whether they do, and in fact reading through the site and familiarising yourself with their work in advance is a good plan, as you're not going in "cold".

You'll stand a much greater chance of them accepting you if you have thought through the sort of subject areas you could cover, perhaps even going so far as to propose a specific article you'd like to write for them.

Blogs thrive on content, and the biggest challenges most bloggers face are coming up with new ideas, and actually having time to write them up; so you'll undoubtedly find that your offer to do their job for them will be welcomed positively!

Most blogs which regularly accept contributors tend to "reward" them with links to your website, and in many cases an extra block of content containing information about you and your business - again adding to both your personal branding, profile-building efforts and of course, your SEO.

Milk your content

70

The key to successful online marketing is, without question, a sound content strategy. Information, entertainment, conversation - these are the cornerstones of what fuels the web, and by catering to these as part of your marketing strategy you'll find online strategy far more effective.

The problem, however, is that it's very easy to run out of things to say! After you've furiously written articles covering every element of your industry from every possible angle, what do you write next?

The trick is to milk your content, for all it's worth. If you've written a fantastic article, why only get one use out of it?

I recently wrote an article called "5 harsh realities about your website", which I started with the intention of it being a single blog post. However, when I'd finished writing I realised it was too long for that, so instead I split it into 5, each "point" as separate posts which were published on my blog over the course of a week.

I also turned it into a 20 minute presentation which I've now delivered 4 times to different business networking groups; as well as a 2 minute video, which is an extremely abridged version of that presentation.

As if that wasn't enough, I also posted it on Tumblr, which is where I put more personal posts, and because of that I was able to add a few lines before the link explaining my motivations behind the original article. During the course of the week in which the series was published, I tweeted lines from it, with a link to the full post; and now here I am, milking it even further by talking about it in this book.

How many people would have just posted that one article and be done with it?

We don't all have the time to write endless amounts of content; we don't want to constantly have to scrape around for new blog ideas. Milk your content, get as much mileage and value from it as possible.

Video Blogs and Webcasts

71

There's a good reason why YouTube is the second largest search engine online; video is a fantastic medium for getting your message out there and, thanks to improvement in Internet connection speeds and wider support for video on mobile devices, it's an area which continues to grow in popularity.

Written content is fantastic, but video gives you that extra special something which goes beyond the written word. Not only does it enable people to put a face on your message, but it also helps that message get across more effectively, ensuring that tone and personality which can be difficult to convey in writing makes it through to your audience.

It's easier than ever to produce videos of high enough quality for your audience too. My personal preference is using a Flipcam, which allows you to record video, tweak it with their simple editor, and upload directly to YouTube. If you don't have a Flipcam, many mobile devices can do the same these days too, at a reasonably decent quality - though a standalone device is typically more fit for purpose.

If writers block is getting in the way of you producing blogs and articles, video is also a great way of achieving the same impact with less content. People typically won't watch a video longer than a few minutes, so it's actually better practice to have less to say! Of course that doesn't mean you just babble about nothing for a few minutes; but you'll be better off for focusing on a single topic and keeping it concise.

With a solid content strategy you don't need to publish more than one video a week, realistically, and because it's something which is so quick to do you can record a full months worth of content in a single morning - just pick some topics, set the camera away, and start talking!

You can take your videos further too - IT professionals, designers, web geeks etc often publish "screencasts", which are on-screen walkthroughs of them completing a certain task; something which has become so popular now it's replacing the traditional text-based tutorial model. Screencasts are, again, very easy to do - you just need a mic, a computer, a topic and the right software. Camtasia is the best screen recoding software by miles - however that costs money, so my personal alternative tool of choice is a web-based service called Screenr (www.screenr.com) which allows you to record 5 minutes of video at a time, which it then processes and makes available for you to embed on your own site.

It can take a little time to get comfortable in front of the camera, but once you find your rhythm the next step up is to host "webinars" i.e. online "seminars" held in real time, where a group of people tune in live to you delivering a video session - which could be anything from training, to a presentation, to a round table discussion and more. Again this is a fantastic way to promote yourself and raise your credibility, and can easily be worked in as a feature of your package or service.

Given that the popularity of online video is growing alongside the ease with which you can get involved in publishing your own, there really is no excuse not to be doing it to add the extra level to your content strategy.

Viral is a myth

72

Less of a tip, more of a dispelling of misconception...

The amount of times I've either seen or heard customers asking for, or companies advertising, viral videos is astounding. For anyone who doesn't know what this means, it means a video (or other piece or content) which reaches mass popularity due to it being so funny, clever, stunning etc that anyone who sees it instantly shares it with their friends.

It's certainly a mouth-watering prospect, but it's a fallacy...

The best viral content became viral completely by accident - a home video of a young boy being bitten by his baby brother, a clip of a panda sneezing, a piano-playing cat; at no point did the creators of those videos approach a marketing company and ask them to make their video "go viral".

There are, of course, corporate examples which have been successful; T-mobile's massively popular videos of musical numbers at an airport, and Cadbury's drum playing gorilla stand out amongst the crowd - but consider the sort of budgets these people had and their capacity to create something you simply don't see every day.

Even with those there was no guarantee, and they both had their first outing as TV adverts before they went viral online. Out of all of the TV adverts these companies produced, and all of the money they throw into this area, those two examples represent a small success rate when it comes to creating something viral, and both companies have tried and failed to replicate that since.

The big problem lies in that concept of "creating something viral" - the viral nature of a video or piece of content is actually completely out of your control; and very rarely does something contrived ever gain that sort of popularity.

The myth that a company can simply conjure up something which is viral is one which irritates me to no end. It's tantamount to saying "I want you to create a product that everyone will buy and then convince a dozen of their friends to buy" - it's all a bit pie in the sky. But that doesn't stop companies offering the creation of viral campaigns as a service.

So yes, please do go out there and record videos, create content, and try to be imaginative when you do so - but don't bank on, or pin your strategy to, the notion that you can manufacture viral content out of thin air, as it's a complete myth.

QR confusion

73

One of my biggest bugbears this past couple of years has been the rise in the use of QR codes. These things have been around for years, although it's interesting how many people seem to think they're a brand spanking new innovation. I do think they are useful, specifically for tying your offline marketing to your online marketing; increasingly so with the rise in the use of Smartphone's which make QR code scanning much easier than it previously was. The thing I can't quite wrap my head around is the rise in people placing their QR codes online.

When you consider that the most popular use of a QR code is to give people a straightforward way of accessing a website link from an offline source, why on earth would you place it on an online source? I've seen people with QR codes on forum signatures, banner adverts, even in actual web pages! Furthermore, all the QR codes do is link through to a URL...

Are people seriously expecting users to go online, visit a website, see a QR code, take out their mobile, scan the code from their monitor and then view that link on their mobile phone? Why would you bother? Where is the sense in that? If you want people to click a link on your website... use an actual link, perhaps? Think about it... seriously.

A lot of it stems from a complete misunderstanding of what QR codes are for, and what they can do. I like to think of them as a physical URL, a tangible "link" that can be used in the real world. With that in mind having them on billboards, big screens at festivals, on packaging, leaflets etc make sense (as long as there's a point to them and it's not just being done because someone said it was the latest cool thing!).

However QR codes can do so much more than just link to a web page. They can enable you to download contact details, create a text message or email, or even prompt the receipt of an SMS message - so many people are either unaware of these potential uses, or simply don't utilise them.

QR code usage is likely to rise in the coming year or so, and I have my fingers crossed for this increase in use to coincide with people starting to realise how best to use them from a marketing context. Hopefully you reading this has helped me do my small part towards making that happen!

Social Media

15 years ago, if you asked somebody to "text" you, you'd no doubt be met with a blank stare. Now, however, sending a text message is something we all do without giving it a second thought.

The introduction of text messaging into everyday life happened almost overnight. The same can be said for Social Media. Regardless of whether you, personally, are an active user of Social Media tools; it is hard to ignore the vastly-increasing part it now plays in day-to-day life.

Social Media is not a fad, it's not a bandwagon, it's not the "next big thing" - it's here, now, and it's here to stay.

The biggest mistake many business owners who approach social media make is failing to realise that these tools were not intended as sales or marketing tools but that they were created, and are predominantly used, as a social medium.

This does not, however, mean that they have no use for your business – far from it!

As a representative of a business, the true power of Social Media lies in its ability to connect you, directly, to your audience – whether they're potential customers, existing customers, or key contacts within your industry. No answering machines, no receptionist gatekeepers – a direct line to the people you want to talk to, and to the people who want to talk to you.

Think about that for a second in terms of how powerful such a resource could be? Without leaving the comfort of your office, or even your living room, you have an open channel to anyone you want to communicate with. Powerful stuff!

The key to Social Media is in identifying what you can use it for and, more importantly, how best to use it to achieve your business goals; something we're going to take a look at in this section...

The art of engagement

74

The use of the Internet as a means to promote your business has sky-rocketed during the course of the past 5 or so years; and the recent evolution of the web towards an environment dominated by social media has led to a surging increase of business owners finally sitting up, paying attention, and trying to figure out how to harness its power to best promote their products and services. This has, unfortunately, created a raft of problems – as countless self appointed "guru's" are now lining up to fill the heads of business owners with talk of "Twitter Strategies" and other such nonsense. In truth, the social web is a simple thing – it's just been overcomplicated by other people.

Interruption Marketing is dead. Consumers no longer want you interrupting their favourite TV program with a commercial; nor do they want your newspaper advertisement distracting them from the article they're reading. We have now entered an age of "Engagement Marketing" where the onus is on getting out there and connecting with your market. People don't want to deal with faceless companies anymore – they want to deal with people.

The problem occurs, however, when business owners are confounded by the various "experts" waving their strategies and 18-month social media action plans into thinking that the Internet is the new medium for Interruption Marketing, and begin trying to find the most effective ways to sell to their customers, rather than to engage with them.

The big clue about Social Media is in its name – it's Social. In the "real world", if you were to wander into a business networking event, or even into your local pub, and start reeling off your sales pitch and ramming your business card down people's throats, it simply would not work. If however, you engage with the people around you, get to know them a little, mention what you do but don't hard sell, and attempt to forge a genuine connection – then ultimately the results will come.

Adopt this same approach and mentality online when utilising the vast and varied tools of Social Media, and you should do just fine.

Connect your social media channels

75

Social Media is, without doubt, the biggest topic in marketing to crop up in the last few years. To an extent it's become a bandwagon or sorts, in the same way that SEO was a few years ago, however that doesn't mean it's without merit - to the contrary, it is exceptionally powerful if harnessed correctly.

While I'm not going to deliver a sermon about social media or quote lines from the famous "Social Media Revolution" video which every other social media "guru" trots out (look up that video, though, if you haven't seen it already) - the tip I will give you is about the practical use of this vast array of social media tools we have at our disposal in terms of tying everything together.

I've come cross a lot of people who put a lot of time, thought and effort into using social media, but they're missing a trick by failing to link all of these channels together. The most valuable currency in terms of online marketing is content, so if you're blogging, you need to be tweeting out links to those blog articles; posting links to your articles on your company Facebook page, setting up your LinkedIn page to display your latest blog articles and so on, and so on!

Twitter, Facebook and LinkedIn all have options or services which automatically show, for example, every one of your tweets in your Facebook or LinkedIn stream, or will automatically tweet your Facebook status etc. Personally I'm not a huge fan of this, or others who do it, as I end up seeing the same stuff over and over again; or see Facebook's more "organised" approach to conversations overridden by a slew of throwaway syndicated tweets.

My personal preference is either to do it manually, or to be smarter about the automation side. If you use Wordpress, for example, to blog, there are plug-in's available that will automatically tweet out the link to your latest article. You can also use services like ittt.com (short for "if this, then that") to handle some of the automation of what happens when you, for example, add a video to YouTube or publish a photograph on Flickr

Additionally there are popular software options such as Hootsuite and Tweetdeck which enable you to manage multiple accounts across a number of different social media services with ease - meaning you have no excuses!

There are a whole bunch of ways in which you can connect your social media activity from one channel to another, to your website, to your blog etc. Wordpress plugin's such as "Auto Tweet" enable you to automatically tweet out links to new blogs items which you post; and services such as Buffer (www.bufferapp.com) enable you to manually schedule future tweets and posts to LinkedIn and Facebook.

While going down the fully automated route isn't my particular cup of tea it's preferable to not connecting things up at all; and there's a massive difference between automating and scheduling.

As I've mentioned numerous times, content is currency, and social media is the best way of getting that content out - something which will have a much greater level of impact if you tie it all together.

DIY Facebook pages

76

I'd imagine there is little point in trying to convince you that when it comes to marketing your business online, Facebook is a pretty big deal. After all, when you consider that it's used by over 845 million people from all walks of life worldwide, I would hope I'm preaching to the converted.

When it comes to Facebook for business, we really need to be looking at their Pages feature. These incorporate a lot of the elements which a personal profile has, such as info, photos, a "wall" etc; but with a business slant. Additionally unlike personal profiles, you can add custom sections and pages too.

Setting up a basic business page on Facebook is a doddle, and doesn't differ too greatly to setting up a regular profile. You can enter blurb about your business, your address, opening times etc, as well as add photographs and your logo. If you're a little savvier you can search for "applications" which you can add to your business page to show your blog feed and YouTube videos with the click of a button. Now you can even choose a custom web address for your page from the getgo (like facebook.com/bootstrapmarketinguk - cheap plug!) – a feature you previously needed to have 50 "fans" to access.

Add on to that the ability to have a discussion forum, as well as a reviews section, and you have a pretty powerful platform for promoting your business on the largest western social networking site.

There are many companies who will charge you for setting up a Facebook page, who can create custom sections with more interactivity specific to your company. That can be great, however if you're working on a budget then don't let the absence of this sort of feature put you off setting up a

Facebook page altogether as even using the "basic" tools Facebook give you by default can help you to build a thriving page, provided you put the work in and promote it as well as interact with your fans and followers.

Once you're all set up then you might consider using a third-party application to create a custom section of your page. Pagemodo (www. pagemodo.com) lets you set up custom tabs, "Like-gates" (where you only show content to people who "like" your page) and a variety of other features. They do have a free plan so if you can live with a big "powered by Pagemodo" image at the bottom you can set this up at no cost.

If you absolutely cannot live without a custom section on your Facebook page but don't want to use a third party, then consider doing it yourself. A basic custom tab consists mainly of HTML and images; and with a quick Google search and a little bit of reading it shouldn't take too much to learn how to cobble together something fairly quickly. Obviously it won't be the bee's knees but if it adds a little something extra at no cost then that can only be a good thing!

Build your social capital

77

"I tried Social Media, doesn't really work…"

I've heard this said quite a few times by quite a few people – they've heard that Social Media is the new "big thing" in marketing your business, and as such have pushed themselves into spending a few hours on it, before dismissing it as a waste of time because they didn't see results.

Typically, however, the people who claim social media does not work are often those who try to extract value from it without putting any in themselves.

It's a little twee, so bear with me through this cheesy analogy; but Social Media is a bit like a bank account. If you don't deposit money into your account, then you can't exactly expect the ATM to start spewing £50 notes when you visit it.

What we're talking about here is "social capital". I like to think of social media as a place where people exchange "value" – in that what I tweet, blog, post on Facebook etc may hold some value to someone, somewhere. Value, of course, means different things to different people – for some, they may find value in the information I post on my blog; it may give them food for thought, insight or tips into the subject that I write about. For others, they may find comedic value in some of the random comments I publish on Twitter; whereby others might see a measurable value in terms of visitors to their website when I share their link or comment with my own followers etc.

If you seek to provide value to those with whom you engage through social media, then you'll find that it's much easier to call on those same people when you are in need of something.

Relationships don't happen overnight, nor does the accumulation of your "social capital". You can't burst onto the social media "scene" and expect people to start bending over backwards to help you – you need to put a little bit in first.

This is where most people get it wrong; they rush up to that Social Media ATM without first depositing anything in their account. Work on providing value and building up your social capital, and you'll soon find it easier to withdraw when needed.

Nosey twits

78

Twitter has done a great many good things since its arrival on the social media scene, but perhaps one of the best is its amplification of a single truth shared by all of mankind... We're bloody nosey!

This is magnified on twitter because of the unique way in which conversations and communication flows. Things go by so quickly that if somebody sees a link posted by someone they know, or accompanying a message that grabs their attention, they'll be far more inclined to click it than they would if you, for example, posted it on a forum.

This isn't because people are more switched on or attentive when it comes to twitter; it's because things move so quickly that they're worried they're missing out on something! This is, of course, a sweeping generalisation, but in principle it highlights Twitter as an extremely powerful means of sharing content and links.

Before you rush off, this doesn't mean you just sit there blasting out links and everyone will click them out of curiosity - social media just doesn't work like that; but if you've taken the time to engage with your followers and to post interesting tweets, then when you do throw out a link to something, or a "salesy" tweet, the combination of hyper-nosiness and recognition of you as someone they've engaged with is a potent one.

Get in to Google+

79

It was only a matter of time until Google stepped into the social media scene. Indeed they've tried a variety of different initiatives in the past, however having gone a little too far off kilter from the rest of the social media movement, in 2011 they went back to basics and unveiled Google+.

While viewed purely as a social media platform, it was relatively underwhelming at launch, missing some key features that people had become accustomed to; but slowly and surely they continued to develop it, building up followers along the way who were drawn by the less cluttered, cleaner and more accessible alternative to the hustle and bustle of Facebook and Twitter.

Some of the features of Google+ hold phenomenal potential, particularly "Hangouts"; organised video chatroom's held on the Google+ website and integrated with your social platform. Already people have started utilising these to deliver webinars, virtual meetings and online business networking meetings.

However it's not the features which make Google+ the new "must join" social network; it's how it relates to the other products in Google's stable, particularly – and quite obviously – search.

In late 2011, Google revealed what will clearly have been their masterplan all along; tweaking their search algorithms and results so that your activity on Google+ now has a direct impact on search engine listings. Not only will your Google+ profile potentially show up in search results; but content that you have shared (i.e. if you post links to your blog articles on your Google+ profile) will now also be shown on result pages.

The twist – and the reason why Google are able to justify what some see as self-serving manipulation of their search engine – is in the idea of "personalised search results". Someone in your Google+ network (or "circles", as they call them), will now be more likely to see content which you have shared or otherwise endorsed than they will other listings. The idea being that you'll have more interest in something your friends expressed an interest in.

This is a new development for search engines, but an enormous one not to be overlooked; and is currently the single most compelling reason for making sure that you and your business join and make use of Google+

Knowing Google, this is only the beginning, so make sure you jump onboard!

Listen to the crowd

80

Stefan Thomas of NoRedBraces (www.noredbraces.co.uk) neatly sums up social media as "a conversation which is taking place whether you're part of it or not" - however this notion is often lost on people who cannot grasp the concept that there may be people out there discussing them and their business without them having a say in what's being said.

Often this means they fall asleep at the wheel, and despite having gone through the motions of setting up a corporate Twitter account or Facebook page, and sticking the office intern or the junior PR consultant at helm, the conversations people are having about them simply pass them by.

My favourite personal experience of this all revolves around pizza...

I do enjoy a good pizza, and when it comes to takeaways, Dominos are far and away my favourite (I blame their ridiculously addictive garlic sauce). When I lived in central Newcastle I was only around 5 miles from the nearest store, and ended up on first name terms with their delivery drivers. However when I moved to the outskirts, despite actually being closer to my local store, they refused to deliver, saying I was outside of their delivery zone.

This infuriated me far more than it should do any relatively sane person, and as they say, squeaky wheels make the most noise, and squeak I did!

I'd moaned about my pizza predicament a couple of times before on Twitter, but one evening I was particularly enraged, and began a one man crusade for justice, tweeting my outrage for all to see, and lobbying the Dominos UK twitter account to try to get their attention.

I finally got a reply from a sympathetic soul who wanted to solve my crisis. However that reply didn't come from Dominos, no, it came from Papa John's, who just so happened to be local to me too, though I hadn't realised at the time.

Someone manning their Twitter accounts was clearly on the ball and was looking for anyone complaining about their rivals. They wasted no time in finding out where I was, confirming that they delivered, and dispatching one of their delivery guys to me with a large pepperoni pizza free of charge. Needless to say, Papa John's ended up getting all of my business from that day forward - all due to a free pizza and someone in their company paying attention where Dominos weren't.

Of course I tell that story with an intentional level of melodrama; however it's just one of many examples big and small of how keeping your finger on the pulse of social media can reap dividends.

LinkedIn's hidden gems

81

LinkedIn is often viewed by many as the forgotten social network. With over 135 million members it's hardly a shrinking violet, however more often than not while people will talk about what they've seen on Twitter or Facebook, LinkedIn tends to be the site which people are members of, know about, but don't tend to use or even know what to do with.

Much of this is no doubt due to the level of activity these sites encourage, and the amount of effort it takes to get involved. Twitter is fast moving, short-blast conversation; Facebook is digital voyeurism; while LinkedIn is seen as something of a digital CV, and think about it, how often do you update your real CV?

As such, so many people sign up to LinkedIn, complete most of their profile, and then forget it for a few months.

I'd imagine many of you reading this book know exactly what I'm talking about, however if you do more than just scratch the surface you'll find that LinkedIn has some seriously useful and powerful hidden gems.

The first is in the comprehensiveness of your LinkedIn profile. In addition to adding employment and educational background, LinkedIn do a great job of showcasing testimonials, and enabling you to ask others to leave them for you. There's also a bunch of great add-ons which you can display on your profile page - from embedded slideshows, portfolios for designers, a round-up of your blog posts, a section for posting and promoting upcoming events, even a reading list to show off how well read you are! All of this showing on your individual profile page, and fully customisable. LinkedIn go way beyond the capabilities of Facebook and Twitter in terms for how you can use your personal profile page to promote your business.

The second gem is in connections. Unlike Facebook you don't just add a friend, you add a connection. You can then view who your connections are connected to, and others can see you too. So if you were to contact somebody, they'll be able to see how you're connected to them. This is the closest any social media site has come to truly representing the core concept of a network that goes deeper than the usual single layer most others do; and has a whole "six degrees of separation" vibe to it. This enables you to explore the full reach of your network, and to apply the concept of "through the room" to social networking.

The third and, in my opinion, most powerful hidden gem of LinkedIn is also the one that's most tucked away, and that's the Questions and Answers section where millions of business people are actively seeking assistance with subjects spanning the entire spectrum of the business world. If you're not tapping into this as a way to prove your expertise, develop an international reputation and make new connections then you're truly missing a trick. Every question you answer has the potential to be rated or voted for by others, and there's a record of your activity levels to show others that you're a knowledgeable, helpful person worth connecting with. And, of course, every time you answer a question, your answer links through to your profile, which helps to bolster the positive first impression you've made. What's more, of you get involved in this side of the website, it gives you a reason to remember to actually use LinkedIn rather than fall into the trap so many others do of thinking social media consists solely of Facebook and Twitter.

So, if you nodded in agreement when I referred to LinkedIn as the "forgotten network", or if you use it regularly yet didn't realise these hidden gems exist, then make sure you take the time to dig a little deeper.

Promoting your business

Let's leave the Internet behind now and get back to the real world – something many marketers these days fail to do. It's easy to become enamored with new technology and online trends, but we shouldn't forget that there's a glut of tried and tested "traditional" marketing activities that can be utilized for little to no cost, and to great effect.

Of course these days, with so many people online, the art of promoting your business offline through more conventional means is something a lot of people struggle to do. Chatting away to someone behind a keyboard can be far less daunting than knocking on the door of a potential client without invitation!

However the key thing to remember is that whether it's online or offline, it's all marketing! You are still dealing with people and products – it is just the medium which changes.

We've experienced something of a perfect storm recently – in that advances in technology and the rise of social media have coincided with a shift in attitudes and approach within the world of business, particularly small business. Whether one is the result of another is something for much smarter people than I am to discuss and assess, but what it means is that we can approach "old school" promotional activities (such as Business Networking) with a "new school" mentality.

I mention elsewhere in the book that we have entered an age of engagement marketing, as opposed to interruption marketing, and while this is typically viewed in the context of social media and online activity, it's true of offline, traditional marketing too.

This creates an environment which is perfect for small businesses, and if you can shake off the apprehension and bad habits typically associated with traditional promotional activities, then you can start seeing real results for your business.

Be a gatecrasher

82

Exhibitions or trade shows, particularly the larger ones targeted at a specific industry or market, can be a great source of new customers. Unfortunately this usually comes with quite a high price tag.

One tactic which really made me smile was adopted by a client of mine who had just set up a training company. They didn't have the budget to afford the hefty cost of exhibiting at a local event, so they attended as a visitor which was free of charge, and went armed with jacket pockets stuffed full of their leaflets. They then proceeded to sneakily leave these leaflets in the coffee areas and promo tables throughout the venue.

This strategy netted them a dozen new clients from over 30 enquiries on the back of their tactics. While they most certainly would have attracted more had they had a table at the event, this was a fantastic result that didn't cost them a penny; and the income from the clients they got from gatecrashing enabled them to pay for a stand at the next event.

Obviously this approach wouldn't work for everyone, as it requires a lot of front, and would be extremely embarrassing if you were caught; so if you don't want to go that far then perhaps consider sharing space at an exhibition with someone who offers a complimentary service to yours.

A photographer, for example, may look to share exhibition space with a wedding planning company; a web designer may pair up with a marketing company etc. Whether it's a case of splitting the costs, or trading your time/services in exchange for a place at their table, it's certainly worth considering if exhibiting alone isn't an option.

Offer commission

83

Finding ways of working with businesses that provide products or services complimentary to your own is a great way of establishing steady streams of enquiries. An easy way to start is to consider offering commissions or incentives for introductions.

Sure, in an ideal world people will refer clients to you due to a genuine and impartial desire to do so, not because they stand to gain financially from it, but let's be realistic here, it's not an ideal world, and while those relationships will happen, if you're comfortable with the idea of commissions it would be foolish to sit around waiting for the call when offering commissions could secure the passing of leads earlier.

My two favourite ways of doing this are a) offering discounts/commissions to existing customers for successful referrals, and b) targeting companies within your industry offering complimentary services and offering them a commission if they upsell your product or service to their client base.

It's that last one where the big potential lies. If, for example, you're a photographer, then it would be mad not to speak to wedding planners, dress shops etc and carve out a commission arrangement.

For those of you worrying about this being an impersonal approach, don't panic, you'll find that even when offering incentives, your potential partners will still only refer to you if they are convinced of your quality, as a small commission to them is no substitute for their own reputation.

Trade services

84

One of the most common complaints I hear from small business owners in terms of them feeling unable to market themselves effectively is that they do not have the budget they need to put their plans into motion.

This is understandable, in the early days most small businesses are time-rich and cash-poor. The solution? If you can't invest cash, invest time!

Chances are that you have a counterpart in the same financial situation who offers what you need, and who needs what you offer, so why not look in to trading services with them?

Not only could this mean you get the resources you need to market yourself (printed assets, banner stands, advertising space etc), but technically the person you have bartered with is a client, even if they haven't paid you in cash, so there's someone else who can sing your praises, provide repeat or referred custom, give you a testimonial etc.

Roller banners
- prominent placement

85

I'd never come across the use of roller banners in networking until I attended my first meeting with 4Networking. I automatically assumed they cost a lot of money, due to their size and the impact they have.

As it turns out I ended up getting my first one from my local printer for under £100 and it lasted me a couple of years. Pretty early on I cottoned on to the fact that during these meetings, people would primarily be looking in the direction of the person running the meeting, and thereby by placing my banner within close proximity of the meeting chair I was stealthily grabbing more attention.

Most other people would pop their banners up wherever seemed most convenient, however putting just that extra little bit of thought into it at your next networking meeting, exhibition or event can pay off.

The power of props

86

The thing to remember when networking is that a large chunk of people in the room are nervous or not comfortable in that sort of environment. Because of this, when it comes time (as it does in a lot of the main networking organisations) to go around the room and give your elevator pitch, most people have their concentration squarely on what it is they are going to say themselves.   You need to get their attention.

Some people do this by screaming and shouting, others with a repertoire of funny jokes - but neither is suited to the average business person. The most effective attention-getters I've seen in networking circles are props. Props can be used either to hit home a certain point or theme; or as something you always have with you to support a gimmick.

My award for favourite prop use goes to a solicitor named Phillip Stephenson, who over the Easter period in 2010 delivered a series of brilliant elevator pitches during which he described his companies services using a lot of words beginning with "ex-", however what Phillip did was to walk around the room, placing a Cadburys Crème Egg in front of an attendee every time he said a word beginning with "ex-…", which with emphasis became "eggs-…" So "eggs-isting clients getting eggs-ellent service from an eggs-tremely good solicitor" saw 3 fellow networkers with a chocolate treat on that table.

This received a rapturous reception, and word quickly spread around the network, drawing a lot of attention to this person and their company, and prompting more leads and enquiries for him than he'd had in the preceding months. Phillip is actually quite a quiet, reserved man - proof that you don't have to be an attention-seeker to get attention!

Keep it simple

87

Not too long ago, a company I worked with were contracted by a restaurant owner to produce a simple leaflet for their already-successful restaurant. The owner of this restaurant had built it from the ground-up, and having experienced a large amount of growth in a short space of time was gearing up to expand into a chain of several similar restaurants in the area.

Nervous at this prospect, the proprietor had started to involve outside consultants to help his business, one of whom was a self-professed marketing "expert". As a bit of background, I knew this "expert", he was one of those self-styled entrepreneurs who had run "dozens" of businesses; something he touted often in his own promotion, glossing over the fact that this meant he had also failed with "dozens" of businesses.

I digress...

What should have been a simple promotional brochure, utilising the beautiful imagery provided by the client and promoting his very attractive offers turned into a hard slog; his marketing expert apparently determined to strip all sense and logic from the process.

At the point at which my designer friend suggested this client go elsewhere, the simple leaflet had turned into a soulless black and white wall of text, devoid of any imagery or branding, and packed with convoluted instructions for the reader.

The marketing "expert" expected recipients of the leaflet to visit a special web address, where they could download a brochure which would not only tell them more about the restaurant, but also give them a discount code which, if they called the restaurant, would result in them being sent a voucher entitling them to a discount from their bill.

So now not only was the leaflet bland and boring, it was now an instruction manual for the most convoluted promotional offer ever. Surely the simpler thing to do would be to include the coupon in the leaflet itself?

"Well that way we don't get to capture their contact details when they download the brochure and call the restaurant"

No, but you get bums on seats and cash in the till.

Sometimes it's better to just keep it simple.

Go door knocking

88

Quite often it's easy to get so wrapped up in all of the newfangled marketing avenues which seemingly open up every day that we forget the old school, proven techniques which were effective years before the first Tweet was sent.

One of the most basic of those forgotten techniques is to lace up your boots and start knocking on some doors!

This won't be the best option for everyone, and isn't for the faint of heart, but with a bit of gusto and thick skin it can prove itself one of the easiest ways to bring in new business.

If you work in or use one of the many serviced office blocks out there, or are based on an industrial park or anywhere else where your neighbours are primarily other businesses; find out a little about them, and then go and knock on their door! You don't need to go in there all guns blazing trying to close a deal before your foot is in the door, but by simply going round, introducing yourself, letting them know what you do and leaving your card; you are one step further in to a whole bunch of new relationships.

You may strike lucky and happen across someone who has a specific need for what you're offering - but don't bank on it. However, next time you pass someone you've met you can stop and have a chat without it seeming odd; all the while helping to burn your name into their mental Rolodex so that when an opportunity arises they know who to speak to.

A printer I used to do a lot of work with years ago did this. His company was based on a massive sprawling industrial estate, and at the time he had some seriously good deals on business cards which he was trying to build capacity for. So off he went around the estate, and after as many warm welcomes as he had closed doors, he came back with over a dozen orders worth close to £1000; all from a morning of chatting and drinking coffee with people he passed silently every day.

A number of those people went on to become long term and high spending clients since they now knew that this company was on their doorstep, and had met and chatted to their representative.

If you don't work in an office or anywhere near an industrial estate, hop in the car and spend a morning doing the rounds! Again I'll say this won't necessarily work for every business type and more particularly every personality type, but if you're a little ballsy and can handle rejection and blank stares from those people who inevitably will dole them out, then go for it! What have you got to lose other than a little bit of leather from your shoes?

Everyone loves free stuff

89

People love free stuff, and I'm not ashamed to admit that I'm one of those people! Giving away a freebie, with your logo on it, of course, can be a great way of winning customer loyalty, and keeping you and your brand as part of their day to day lives.

My personal favourite freebies? Pens. I love free pens, can't get enough of them! I've got a stash of various companies pens tucked away in the top drawer of my desk and whenever I'm at networking events, exhibitions and trade shows I'm always on the prowl for more! Same goes for notepads too, and when I'm doodling away with a branded pen on someone else's branded notepad, I'm getting that constant reminder about those companies.

It's easy to get it wrong with branded items though, you need to give some real thought to what people are actually likely to take away and use. Stress balls, mouse mats, lanyards and the like are a bit of a novelty, but people are far more likely to shove them into the junk drawer (or the bin) than they are, say, a branded mug.

Quality is important though, if your branded pen falls to pieces when I try to use it, then this paints your company as being as cheap and flimsy as that pen!

Of course you could end up spending a fortune on this sort of stuff, so it's something you may want to leave until you have a budget behind you - however in the meantime with a bit of creativity you can still achieve the same effect.

My favourite "out there" freebie came courtesy of one of my favourite web geeks Neil Pie (www.neilpie.co.uk). Neil is quite a quirky guy anyway so can get away with certain things, such as delivering a 60 second pitch at a networking event which consisted mostly of him drinking a cup of tea, and using frozen peas and a bottle of HP sauce in his video blogs. His top stroke of genius, however, was in him offering up a free cut out mask of his own face to everybody who "liked" his Facebook page over a 2 week period.

It's such a ludicrous idea that it actually worked! The fact Neil had crazy hair and a bit of a wild beard made the whole thing even funnier and he's still remembered for it to this day.

Again this is one of those things that won't work for everyone, but is an example of the sort of results you can get just from using a bit of creativity. It doesn't have to be quirky or whacky either, just a slight twist on the norm. This year, instead of sending out Christmas cards, my friends at the Media Partnership sent out branded chocolate advent calendars along with their seasonal print catalogue. That means someone would be giving daily attention to something with their logo on for an entire month, and every time they walked over to that Media Partnership logo, they came away happy. That's a great feeling to have associated with your brand!

So keep in mind just how well free stuff tends to work, put some thought into whether people will actually use or respond to your freebies, and try a little creativity to help you to stand out.

Delicious documents

90

Marketing isn't just about flyers, fancy logos and painfully crafted strategy documents; every time you make some form of connection with a client, prospect or innocent bystander is an opportunity to create a positive impression.

Despite this I see a lot of companies which have amazing websites and water-tight promotional campaigns turn a blind eye to the little things, like the documents and paperwork they send out to their clients. If your dazzling brochure has struck the right chord and landed you a new client, how daft is it for your proposals, contracts and letters to look like they've been cobbled together by a trained chimp with a typewriter?

Since we're going "bootstrap" here, it's pretty apt to say that most people reading this book, unless you're in the design industry, won't have copies of software like Photoshop (legal ones at least), but I'd daresay most of you will have some sort of desktop publishing package like Microsoft Office. If you use this to create documents for use in your business, then it's not too difficult for even the biggest luddite to create something a little more impressive than the typical boring wall of text.

For a start you should be making sure all your documents are branded with your logo - you can use company colours but personally I think keeping everything black and white/greyscale looks classier and avoids the risk of your printouts looking cheap when you run then off from your nephew's Bubble-jet printer.

For proposals, space things out a bit and divide them into sections. Not only does this make them easier to read (and therefore more likely to actually be read), but it'll also improve appearance tenfold compared to having a continuous running document. Still on proposals, make sure you have a cover sheet - doesn't have to be anything fancy, just your logo and a brief summary or headers related to the project; this is far better than just sticking "bold" and "underline" on a title at the top of a war and peace document.

Experiment with sidebars, columns and spacing; use nice, clear headers, and avoid the temptation to throw in a whole bunch of novelty fonts to try to make your business look quirky. Comic Sans does not make you look cute; it makes you look like a very different 4-letter 'c-word'...

Okay that's a bit harsh, but please, please do not use Comic Sans, ever, on anything!

I'm not saying that every piece of boring documentation has to be a work of art - but you should at least put a little bit of effort into making them look professional. If you're stuck, have a rummage through your drawers for any letters, contracts, quotes etc you've received from larger companies like your bank, for example - just as a measuring stick for what works, and what doesn't.

If you are really stuck then a quick Google search will turn up a whole bunch of free templates for Microsoft Word and it's like for the most common types of documents you're likely to send.

Above all, just remember that even if something isn't strictly part of your "marketing material", it's still sending a message to your customer base, and it's an easy win to make sure that it's the right message being sent.

Contests with context

91

Until recently the only thing I'd ever won in my life was a trip to the Walkers Crisp Factory when I was 11, and so my standard response to pretty much every competition I came across was one of apathy since "I never win anything".

Most of the time it's actually the nature of the prize which is off-putting; throwing my name into a very large hat to win a "holiday of a lifetime" seems like a pointless venture, because that prize is so big, so fanciful and so perfect that I deem it way beyond my chances of winning and therefore not worth bothering with. Same goes for things like the National Lottery, the odds seem way too high for little old me to even consider trying, so I don't. I do, however, play scratch cards; but the odd thing is I go for the ones with, say, a £4000 jackpot, rather than a £250,000 one.

I've had £4000 in my bank before, countless times, and so it's easy to envisage having it in there again as a result of buying a scratch card, whereas I've never had quarter of a million in there, so I don't know what it's like, and therefore as a prize it's not something I can picture myself as having a chance of winning.

Now obviously millions of people do take a punt on the big dream prizes in competitions; but if you are running one yourself then consider the "losing mindset" that many like me view them with when considering what prizes to offer. A contest to win one of a thousand pairs of cinema tickets seems so much more grounded and achievable than winning an all expenses trip to the red carpets of Hollywood.

The problem is that it's not quite as flashy; so the best of both worlds would be to offer the top prize as well as the more realistic runners-up prizes.

If running a competition, consider options for making the chances of winning more realistic, and try offering prizes which fit into the context of your participant's day to day lives. We all pay our mortgage or rent every month - and so a prize of having it paid for you for a year, versus a lump sum prize of the same value seems so much more winnable.

Getting noticed

Unless you've come up with a product, service or concept which is truly unique and which sells itself, chances are that there is a plethora of other people just like you, offering exactly the same thing, at roughly the same price. More likely than not, there's a bunch of them operating in the same area, trying to reach the same audience.

Most sales, marketing and business experts will talk of the need for a USP – a unique selling point – however this is a notion which has become so clichéd that even the quest to be "unique" has become pretty generic! Not because being unique doesn't work – but because people approach it as a tick-box exercise.

Additionally in the quest to find something to help them stand out from competitors, people often look in the wrong place. This is something I see all of the time in the web industry – designers and developers brag of the quality of their coding, the speed with which their sites load, the fact that they use the latest cutting edge technology etc – however in most cases, the average business owner simply doesn't care about any of that! Yes, these are all important things, and if the benefits were explained in terms of how they'll provide tangible results for the client, then perhaps they'd be good selling points – but ultimately people just want to know, in simple terms, how it's going to help or benefit them.

Relying on the features and benefits of your product in order to ascertain a USP is a somewhat tired approach. Instead, getting yourself noticed by making the right sort of noises in the right places, and infusing your own personality into your offering is a far easier way of dividing yourself from the pack.

It is just attention seeking – but you don't need to shout and scream in order to get noticed – just use a bit of creativity and have a hook that helps set you apart. Some of the tips which follow are a little bit out there, they won't work for everything, but, may hopefully help spring forth ideas on how you could put your own spin on things…

Free seminars

92

As the saying goes, everybody has a story to tell, and there is a great deal of value in sharing yours free of charge. That's not to say that you need to go digging out the childhood photo albums and reminiscing about first loves - I'm talking about creating free workshops and seminars related to the products and services you offer.

Before you start rubbing your hands at the prospect of running an hour long sales pitch for your particular type of widget, even when offering a free seminar you have to make sure it has value to your audience as even though they are not giving you cash, they are giving you their time.

On the flip side I'm not suggesting you give away the golden eggs of your business either - but it really shouldn't be a great stretch to provide a free "taster" of sorts where you give away advice, information and guidance while still giving people a reason to want to follow up with you in a way that will make you money.

Educating and informing your potential customers in a way which helps them; demonstrates your expertise and competency; and builds goodwill by providing your time free of charge, is worth its weight in gold.

Furthermore there are a bunch of other benefits too; you'll find that people will be more than willing to offer testimonials, for example, after the seminar - and you can go a step further and actually capture some of those on video, which would hold much greater weight than having them in writing.

And while you've got the Flipcam out, how about having someone record your seminar so you can offer it online in its entirety, or cut together a highlight reel as a basis on which to go on and provide more extensive paid seminars or to secure speaking gigs.

So many people are so protective of their knowledge that the idea of giving any of it away for free would send them running - but there is no doubt that it is a fantastic way to generate goodwill, prove your expertise, raise your profile and so on. Further to this, people are notorious for failing to act on free advice anyway, and so would be more likely to return to you for paid expertise.

The crux of this is the fact that educating and informing your potential customers, as well as putting them in a mindset where they are thinking about things related to what you sell, puts you in a much greater position to establish a business relationship that pays.

Speaking gigs

93

Public speaking is a fantastic way to raise your profile and demonstrate your expertise, so finding your way onto the speaker circuit for business events is a goal that many strive for. However, the reality is that a great number of people compete for a limited number of places on the bill at large events, with those who are truly at the top of their profession or who have a solid business "celebrity" profile making it.

Everyone has to start somewhere, however, and if public speaking is something you want to do there are plenty of ways to get started.

Most organised business networking events include a speaking slot of some sort - some membership based organisations offer this up on a rotation basis amongst its members; whereas for others it's simply a case of putting your name forward with a topic you want to talk about.

Local business events, smaller scale exhibitions and things like the Chamber of Commerce also tend to regularly be on the lookout for speakers and are definitely worth approaching.

You are highly unlikely to get paid for your efforts and chances are you will be talking to a relatively small audience - but it's a start! Not only does it enable you to raise your profile and potentially open up opportunities for larger gigs; but it also gives you a chance to perfect your technique, test out material, and hone your presentation skills.

If you do find yourself being either invited to speak or accepted into a slot you've put yourself forward for, don't screw it all up by penning a 30 minute sales pitch, or worse, putting people through hundreds of boring PowerPoint slides!

If you are going to use public speaking as a means to market your business you need to have something to say, and be able to actually say it! Being nervous is fine, being boring isn't!

This really is something that won't fit each and every personality style, but even the most reserved of people can suddenly find their confidence soaring by using some of the smaller speaking opportunities to broaden their experience and get over the early butterflies by working with a smaller, friendlier crowd.

Not quite 100%

94

This is one of those "out there" tips I mention in the intro, and is inspired by a very small, very specific idea I used. Being a typical geek, I'm a big fan of video games; and several of the first websites I built were centred around this theme. One such website was a messageboard for an online role-playing game which had attracted over 40,000 members. I'd always promoted my messageboard as "100% unofficial", until I realised that the lead developer of the game had signed up as a member of my forum.

This gave me the daft idea of tweaking my branding and promoting the site as being "99% unofficial" – with that missing "1%" being the games staff member (suggesting endorsement without explicitly stating it). From then on I had a handful of people every week or so asking me what the 99% was about – it was quirky and somewhat mysterious enough to compel people to want to find out more.

Now you might think its daft (I did warn you), but I was quite pleased with myself for the simplicity of that, and even if it only resulted in one more person taking an interest in and joining the forum, that's a massive return for the sake of putting "99% unofficial" instead of "100%".

I don't want you lot to suddenly start proclaiming your product as 99% something-or-other; but hopefully what this illustrates is that making such a simple tweak to something which is quite cliché can be enough to grab people's attention and raise their curiosity levels, giving you a quick win!

Have a think about whether you could twist something like the "99%" thing to what you do. "We're 99% better than Joe Bloggs Accountants, but they are better than us at filing tax returns a week late"

Build your own buzz

95

We would all love to be the leading industry expert, that guy who pops up in TV any time your industry is discussed, the name that always seems to appear in newspaper and magazine articles. There's not a lot of room "at the top" though, and often times the people there have either spent a lifetime getting there or they are the fore-runners of their profession.

So while chatting to Jeremy Paxman about the ins and outs of the plumbing industry may not be on the cards for you just yet, how can you go about building the sort of buzz which comes from having your name and picture all over the place?

The first, and easiest step, is to splash yourself all over the first page of Google, so that when people search for your name, you dominate the results. Get yourself a profile on a plethora of social media sites and forums, publish articles on the main article distribution sites, grab your personalised domain name and get a one page profile up, and so on and so on. Now I said this is easy but perhaps that's overstating it - if your name happens to be Brad Pitt then you are buggered, but given that all of these activities have other benefits it's worth doing for a shot at standing out amongst the crowd if people search for your name.

The second step to consider is to set up your own content network - for example a series of blog sites, online forums, weekly podcasts etc all related to different aspects of your industry, which you could easily look to collaborate with others on, and all with their own brand and identity which is completely independent from you and your own business. So when you "big yourself up" as being featured on such-and-such-news.com and a regular guest on BlahBlah Podcast, nobody needs to know that the reason you're featured so heavily is because they are your sites!

Yes, this is nepotism of the highest order, and yes it could be seen as a little bit naughty - however as long as the "stuff" you are putting out there through your newly established soapboxes is quality then it's nothing to be ashamed of, and it's perfectly reasonable to make a song and dance about all of these articles you're having published etc.

The third and final step would be to get out there and throw yourself in to every speaking opportunity, every free magazine looking for articles, every blog or news site which you don't happen to run yourself - no matter how big or small - get yourself out there, take press clippings (which conveniently snip out the fact it's from the Crinkly Bottom Chronicle rather than the Financial Times), get video footage of every speaking opportunity; and then milk it for all it's worth, get it all up on your personal site, online profiles etc.

Before too long you'll find yourself with a whole heap of momentum and people may very well start paying attention and offering you real opportunities. And if they don't, all of the activity you'll have done has a whole heap of other upsides which you'll benefit from –increased profile, establishing credibility, greater search presence and so on.

Do your bit for charity

96

Call me cynical, but by and large I believe there's no such thing as a selfless act. Even the things we do purely out of the goodness of our hearts typically have a "return" of that warm fuzzy feeling of contentment from helping others.

Because of this I don't feel bad about suggesting that we can leverage being charitable as a marketing activity; so long as it presents a win-win situation for all involved.

Charitable acts are great for PR, and while I'm not suggesting we undertake a 10k marathon every weekend in the name of getting business, there are plenty of things we can do to help ourselves by helping others.

A web design company may offer a free website every year to a chosen charity – and build a whole bunch of activity around the selection of that charity (such as using social media to encourage people to nominate a worthy recipient of this free service).

You might consider participating in a traditional type of fund-raising activity such as abstaining from alcohol or another "vice", taking part in a fun-run, or sitting in a bathtub of baked beans for a day; promoting this activity through your business to help you raise cash while also raising your profile.

There are also more passive and consistent activities or policies your company could adopt in order to be charitable. I know plenty of businesses who donate a small percentage of each invoice to a chosen charity; or who give customers the option of "rounding up" their purchase (say from £95 to £100) with the "rounded up" portion going to a worthy cause.

Not only do these sorts of acts build a tremendous amount of goodwill; they give you a story to put out there for potential press coverage, as well as giving you something unique over your competitors as a compelling reason to do business with you.

It doesn't have to cost you a lot of money or time in order to present yourself as a business with a heart – so think about what you could do to leverage charitable activity as a means of marketing your business.

The little things

97

I am a huge fan of "the little things", those small, inconsequential things people do in the everyday running of their business that bring a smile to my face. Whether it's a restaurant who put "Drumstick" lollies on the plate with the bill instead of the traditional mints or small chocolate; or someone who always puts a little handwritten "thanks" on their invoice - I'm a sucker for this stuff, and others are too, and the great thing is that these little touches often cost little or nothing at all.

It's not just the novelty factor either - my better half runs Panacea Natural Health Services (www.panacea-health.co.uk), through which she supplies her own range of health remedies and supplements, oftentimes bespoke to her clients needs. With the bespoke remedies, she has to label the bottles herself; but rather than just scribble something down she prints off the labels, always with her logo in the corner and the text in her company colours. Not groundbreaking, not uncommon, but those extra few minutes it takes to do that help to add that little bit of added polish that goes a long way to strengthening her brand.

If I go to a business networking meeting, it makes the world of difference when there's a printed placeholder with my name and company on it which I can use to set down at my seat - just a bit of card that takes minutes to prepare, but a huge difference maker in terms of making you feel welcome.

Whenever I get a new stationary catalogue from my local stationer there is always a little chocolate inside the envelope (though as luck would have it mine is usually crushed to bits!).

And whenever I book a hotel room with Premier Inn, they always text me a few days before my booking to remind me of the details and give me information for programming my sat nav.

The little things go a hell of a long way to differentiating you from your competitors, and to drum up loyalty and affection from your clients. What little things are you doing to be different?

Demonstrate expertise 98

Some industries are tarnished by the "lower contingent" who jump on the bandwagon to try to make some fast cash without the prerequisite skills. This makes it extremely difficult for legit, quality suppliers to differentiate themselves, as often doing this requires explaining the technical aspects of what they do, which typically bores clients to tears.

Search engine optimisation is most definitely one of those industries. In the mid nineties, website design was the bandwagon, moving into 2000 onwards it was search engine optimisation, and for the past few years it's been social media - however SEO still harbours those poor quality practitioners.

Gareth Mailer runs Clickworks Media, a company specialising solely in SEO, and he's actually pretty bloody good (see his earlier tip "SEO Made Simple" for proof!). However he quickly found himself up against the challenges described above. Furthermore he was trying to carve out a name for himself on a heavily populated online forum where every other person claimed to specialise in SEO.

Rather than giving up and trying a different route, or getting bogged down in boring clients with techy stuff to prove himself, he took a different tactic. Starting with the forum he was posting on, he began posting a series of comprehensive 30 minute long videos analysing the in's and outs of SEO on a variety of fellow forum users websites, complete with in depth advice and guidance on how to improve their performance.

This was initially done without invitation, but he quickly found people lining up to ask him to review their websites. These weren't self-promotional fluff pieces; they were meaty, valuable insights containing the sort of information and advice that most people wouldn't think of giving away for free.

This led to him very quickly establishing himself as a true expert in his field, and a helpful guy to boot; and what was very smart about this approach was that the people whose websites were analysed (I have to add, all of it was constructive, no negativity or bashing) had essentially been given a free 30 minute consultation, and so it was a no brainer for people continue on from that on a paid basis as essentially they were already down the path of using Gareth as their SEO specialist.

The best way to demonstrate your expertise is to actually, y'know, demonstrate it - more often than not the opportunity to do so doesn't come until you are being paid by a client - however by putting yourself out there and investing in doing something like Gareth did, you move that process from behind the closed door of a supplier/client relationship and put it on show for all to see.

Make 'em laugh

99

Laughter is the best medicine, and when it comes to promoting your business it's a powerful thing too! Nobody has ever punched someone in the face for making them laugh, so if you can inject a little humour into proceedings it can go a long way to endearing you to potential customers.

Jan Jack runs Perfect Verse (www.perfectverse.co.uk), a company offering bespoke poetry and writings for a variety of purposes - from gifts, to scripts for promotional pieces. She also runs Laughter-House, a monthly comedy club in Basingstoke which features a plethora of top stand up talent.

Given that it's not a "traditional business" like, say, an accountancy firm or printing company, Jan's proposition can be a tricky one to promote. However, she leverages social media brilliantly, utilising her comedic skills to etch her name in people's minds for the right reason. Several times a day, Jan will tweet funny short poems or jokes in her own unique style, which are almost always guaranteed to get a positive reaction and, most importantly, to be shared by people who read them. Hardly a day passes where I don't have a little chuckle at something she has written; and that only makes me want to read more and find out what she does.

As a result I've now travelled to Basingstoke twice to visit Laughter-House (www.laughter-house.co.uk), and have commissioned Jan to write some pieces which I plan on using while I'm out and about networking for a different twist on the typical 60 second blurb; and I'm not the only one, plenty of others who were first introduced to Jan through her funny tweets have gone on to do business with her too.

You could argue that the nature of what Jan does makes it easy for her to make others laugh in this way, but the same applies to "boring" stuff too.

Few things are quite as boring as a company offering server space; however one such company in the North East attracted a lot of attention with their billboard ad featuring a busty blonde holding a computer server with the tagline "Put your hardware in my rack". Cheesy, yes; smutty, definitely; but in such a gloriously self-aware way that it couldn't fail to raise a titter (come on, that had to be done!)

Of course, not everybody is funny, but many types of industry have their own subculture and stereotypes that make great fodder for a little self-mocking, and of course if you are completely stuck for ways in which to put a funny spin on your ads or your message you can always give someone like Jan a call!

Self publish a book

100

Unless I've been picked up by some huge name publisher (in which case, aloha from my cabin on a Hawaiian beach), this book you are reading has been entirely self-published; and it would be remiss of me not to suggest taking the same route as I did as a good way to market yourself at minimal cost.

They say everyone has at least one decent book in them (I'll leave you to decide whether this is mine!); however historically it has always been a bit of a punt to write a book when the chances of being picked up by a traditional publishing house is about as likely as winning the lottery.

There was, of course, always self publishing; however that came with two main challenges - firstly, the prospect of having to remortgage your house in order to pay for the cost of printing thousands of copies, and secondly the fact that unless you went round secretly slipping copies of your books onto the shelves at Waterstones it was quite difficult to actually distribute books without the backing of a publisher.

Now, however, those challenges are gone.

Print on demand services such as lulu.com have all but removed the risk of needing to order a massive print run of your book. How it works is that each book is printed to order - so if someone buys your book through Lulu, they print off that single copy and mail it out to the customer themselves, the cost for which is deducted from your selling price. Given that an averaged sized book will have print costs of around £3-£4, if you're selling for £10 that's a huge margin compared to what you'd get going down the traditional publishing route, and without the hassle of ever having to get involved in the production and fulfilment side of things.

If you haven't heard of lulu.com and are thinking maybe this whole self-publishing thing is new and a bit shaky, trust me it isn't - lulu.com actually link in to amazon.com too, so they are a big deal, which means that if you opt for it your books can be sold through Amazon's website on the same print-on-demand basis. Amazon themselves do have their own self-publishing arm (www.createspace.com) - though it's very much skewed towards the US market, so it may be best sticking with Lulu for now.

So that's part of the distribution problem handled too - the rest of which is aided massively by the Internet as a distribution channel, particularly thanks to the huge surge in digital books due to the rise in popularity of devices such as the Amazon Kindle and Apple iPad.

Amazon recently reported that for the first time ever, sales of digital books for their Kindle device had surpassed sales of physical books. That is a phenomenal development and one which continues to progress; which makes self publishing through this platform a mouth-watering prospect. Once again the margins here are a heck of lot bigger than traditional publishing, and you can earn royalties of up to 70% of the sale price.

The money side of things isn't important (though it's a nice side effect!); from a marketing perspective, self publishing your own book gives you so many options. For a start it adds a bit of credibility (though admittedly not at as high a level as if picked up by a traditional publishing house); it helps to prove your expertise; it's a low-cost item for people to buy and essentially stands as a cover to cover advertisement and endorsement for you as an expert in your field; and it's a great prop and source of inspiration for you when it comes to crafting presentations and thinking of what to write for blog posts etc.

The list of benefits to writing your own book goes on and on. It's not something you'll do in a weekend (most likely), and it's not something you should really try to blag since people will expect you to have done your best work if you're committing it to paper - and as such if you have just filled your book with junk, they may think that's the best you can do. However it doesn't have to be a chore; you can do it at your own pace, in your spare time.

This book started out as a list I put together using the Evernote application on my Android phone. Any time I had a spare five minutes or a sudden flash of inspiration for different tips I could write, I'd simply add it to the list. When the list got to 70 points, I transferred it to a writing app on my iPad, and just started writing a bit at a time. Finally I built momentum and committed to writing a full tip every night, and then picked up steam and would write 4 or 5 back to back - still using my iPad (which I'm writing on right now!)

As it turns out a friend of mine beat me to the punch with his own book (31 Mistakes Every Online Business Makes by Dickie Armour, check it out at www.31mistakes.co.uk!), which he asked me to help him self-publish. I'd considered setting up a separate project helping people to publish their books under my "label" at a low cost, which I planned to pursue after the launch of Bootstrap Marketing, however Dickie forced my hand! Interestingly, since we launched his book I've spoken to at least a dozen people I know who now want my help publishing their book, and I've not even promoted my own publishing gig yet! Just shows there's huge demand from people wanting to get a book out there.

There really hasn't been a better time to look into self-publishing and it's an area which is going to grow more and more fruitful - so stop putting off that great book idea; close this book, right now, and go away and write at least one paragraph, then go back and write another tomorrow, and another the next day; and when you've suddenly found yourself with a fully written book, come and have a chat with me or check out www.bootstrappublishing.biz!

Enter business awards
by James Millman

101

Since 2011 I have spoken at a number of events about the benefits of entering into business awards. This follows the success JAM had in 2010 when we won several business awards including best medium sized business in Hertfordshire. Below are some of reasons why I firmly believe every small business should enter into a business award.

Raise Your Profile

Winning an Award or just being a finalist gives you the perfect excuse to tell as many people as you possibly can about your achievement. It will add credibility to your business and make people sit up and take notice of your company. Things to consider doing are telling all your clients, using all social media outlets including blogging, twitter, Facebook, LinkedIn, as well as standing up at networking events and telling people. You may also wish to consider employing a local PR company to see if you can be written about in the local business newspapers and magazines.

Award Application Forms

There is so much to be learnt simply from looking at an award application. It may expose gaps in your business you didn't realise, or prompt you into putting something in place which will benefit your business. If you complete an award application it will force you to examine your business very closely and look at exactly how you have achieved certain things. This is a very useful exercise because it will help you plan better for the future.

Business Plans

A common criteria for business awards is to submit a business plan. By entering into an award it offers you the perfect opportunity to either create a new plan or revisit and update an old one. Writing and updating business plans is of course something many business owners tend to neglect as they are too busy with the day to day running of their company.

Boosting Morale

Attending a business awards finals evening is the closest we as business owners will ever get to experiencing what the actors do at the Oscars. Attending an awards finals evening is also the perfect excuse to treat your staff to a great evening out. If you are lucky enough to win the whole team can then share in the joy, and will undoubtedly help boost morale.

James Millman is a director at JAM, the UK's longest running telephone answering service
www.jam.co.uk

Over-deliver

102

Do you see what I did there?

If you ever have an opportunity to over deliver, grab it with both hands, and if the opportunity doesn't exist, create it.

An example of creating the opportunity to over deliver would be if you are designing a logo and business card for somebody and know that it will only take you another hour to add these to a basic letterhead and compliment slip, keep that up your sleeve when talking to the client, and then go ahead and do it. You might be tempted to try to up-sell with these items as extras, or tell the client that you can "throw them in at the same price", but the value of being able to surprise them with more than they were expecting is huge.

You do need to exercise caution and a bit of restraint on two fronts - firstly you need to ensure you're not going so far off script that you risk upsetting the client (i.e. if you've been hired to knock down a kitchen wall, and go ahead and level their garage too I'm sure they'd be slightly annoyed!); and secondly you need to ensure that any over delivery is commercially sound - don't give someone a car just because they bought a bumper sticker!

Over delivery doesn't just have to pertain to giving extra "stuff" for free either. For years whenever I had a client for whom I'd built a custom content management system, part of the service was that I'd write up a reference/ training guide too. More recently, I've scrapped this and started recording half a dozen training videos showing screencasts of me demoing their system.

From the outset they are told I will provide training materials, but because they automatically assume this will be a training manual they are impressed when I give them videos which are not only far more useful for them, but also take me less time to produce!

The easiest way to over deliver is on timescales and service. If you know a job will take two weeks, tell them 3, then when you deliver after 2 they will love you for it! Offer people advice, insight and info where you can; and don't be afraid of showing people how hard you are working for them either - on a few occasions when I've been working late on a project, I've deliberately waited until 2am to email a client something. When they see that email the next day and spot the time, they immediately see just how much effort I'm making, just for them!

Doing a great job is one of the best free ways of marketing yourself positively. Doing an even better job than expected is even better!

Summary

So there you have it, 101 (well, 102) top tips to market your business on a budget. All of these ideas and strategies could work for any business – however chances are only some of them will work for you personally. That personal element is important – not everyone will be comfortable taking on speaking gigs, for example, and there will undoubtedly be many who understand how door-knocking could be effective, but will never consider doing it.

It's not about trying everything in this book; it's about figuring out which you would be willing and able to try, and then taking action. I can't understate the value of pushing yourself outside of your comfort zone, so if there's something you are in two minds about trying then just go for it – the worst that can happen is that it won't work, and even then you'll walk away a little wiser.

The Bootstrap mentality is about working and marketing smarter, not harder – whether you are investing time or money you need to make sure your investments are savvy; and so throwing a whole load of stuff at the wall and seeing what sticks is a sure-fire way to waste a lot of your resources.

Personally I recommend revisiting this book – picking out one tip a day, or one a week, and resolving to take action. If you try to do it all at once, it won't get done. If you read this book then just shove it on the shelf, nothing will get done. It all comes down to you, and your resolve to take action.

I actually hope that a lot of you will have already known, understood, or tried some of the tips and snippets of advice you've read, as that means you are better primed to implement some of the other ideas. But even if you are just starting out or have been muddling along for years without taking marketing action then hopefully there is plenty of information you have read to ignite ideas and prompt you into doing something.

In the end, it all comes down to you – in the metaphorical Dodgeball game of business, are you going to be smart on your toes, stay nimble and manoeuvre the marketing landscape effectively; or are you going to be watching on, beaten and weary, from the sidelines?

It's entirely up to you – get out there, start taking action, start getting results – start Bootstrapping!

Contributors

A huge thank you to the following people for contributing their expertise to this book. I wanted to avoid the laziness of having other people write half of my book and so thought very carefully about who to ask in order to ensure they were adding real value rather than just padding things out.

Tamsen Garrie

From Corporate HR and Operational Management, to self-employed Clinical Hypnotherapist, to Network Director for the UKs largest joined up business network, to owner of Alpha Associates, Tamsen has had a varied career. It was the combination of her business experience, strong leadership and an inherent understanding of people that enabled her to develop the infrastructure, including the leadership team, processes and training materials to enable the significant growth of a small business network in the South West into the national business that it is today.

Tamsen now runs her own business, Alpha Associates where she specialises in business strategy and skills training. Her experience working with hundreds of businesses, training numerous leaders and developing numerous teams has resulted in a thorough understanding of the many challenges that are familiar to business owners. This coupled with her engaging communication style and her ability to work with all types of people makes her uniquely placed to work with businesses to develop the mind-set, the skills and the behaviours necessary to create personal and business success.

www.alpha-associates.biz
www.tamwithaplan.co.uk

Dickie Armour

Dickie is a successful entrepreneur, author and speaker in the fields of online marketing and social media, and also serves as a non-executive director of Nominet and General Manager of Fibranet Services Ltd. Dickie also runs Business Mentors Club and mentors business owners to help them and their businesses be more successful.

Dickie's latest business book is "31 Mistakes Every Online Business Makes" and was also published by Bootstrap Publishing.

www.31mistakes.co.uk
www.dickiearmour.me.uk

James Millman

James watched JAM grow from a two man band (founded and run by his parents) as a small child into one of the UK's leading telephone answering service taking calls on behalf of a wide array of companies of all shapes and sizes.

After a running his own businesses following graduation from UMIST, James became more heavily involved in JAM in 2005, and has driven their continued growth and success over the past 7 years, picking up various awards and accolades along the way.

www.jam.co.uk

Gareth Mailer

Gareth Mailer is a Search Engine Optimisation professional of seven years and owner of Clickwork Media, a UK based SEO Agency. Gareth is a rarity is the industry, forgoing the "baffling with science" approach of so many

SEO practitioners in favour of transparent and highly effective advice and services.

Clickwork Media works to deliver tailored, bespoke SEO solutions including link building packages, SEO training courses and SEO campaigns, with a constant focus on delivering a ROI to an ever-growing number of customers.

www.clickworkmedia.co.uk

With additional thanks to:

Callie Willows, Katie Millman, Mark Bryant, Paul Norman, Karen Orangetree, Neil Pie, Matt Purser, Lee Rickler, Geoff Burch, Brad Burton, Stefan Thomas and everyone who has ever supported me, inspired me, made me laugh or made me think.

Need more top tips?

As a thank you for purchasing this book, I'm inviting you to register your purchase online in order to receive a **Bootstrap Bonus!**

Ten more top tips for marketing your business on a budget, including:

Using Pinterest for business
Developing a Foursquare strategy
Marketing lessons from our American cousins
Getting press attention for your business
and more!

Grab your bonus now at
www.bootstrapmarketing.co.uk/bonus

2253079R00128

Printed in Great Britain
by Amazon.co.uk, Ltd.,
Marston Gate.